The Geometry Wholemovement

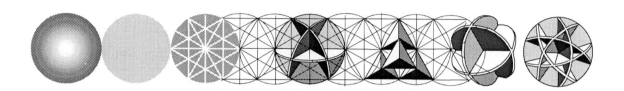

folding the circle for information

Bradford Hansen-Smith

Published by Wholemovement Publications

This book is dedicated to Alexander, Clare, Lily, Maile, Mahala, Henry, and the teachers that will inspire them and their generation towards greater experience and understanding into wholeness.

With much appreciation to Tom Creamer and Melissa Davis for their respective efforts and editing skills, ...and to Grounder, who moves silently...

BH-S

Copyright © 1999 by Bradford Hansen-Smith
All Rights of Reproduction Reserved

Library of Congress Catalog Number 99 96944

Revised First Edition

All drawings and writing were done using Microsoft Word 5.0 and 7.0 on a Gateway 2000

Cover image: "Double Spiral", a digital photography of a sculpture using 31 folded circles. The folded form used for the sculpture is found on page 121.

Published/Distributed by;
Wholemovement Publications
4606 N. Elston, #3, Chicago IL, 60630 , USA
(773) 794-9764 e-mail brad@synasoft.com
The Copy Workshop
(773) 871-1179 Fax 773-281-4643

Also by Bradford Hansen-Smith

The Hands-on Marvelous Ball Book
Published by Books for Young Readers, Scientific American, W. H. Freeman & Co./ New York 1995
Distribution handled by Wholemovement Publications

This book presents a new and unique approach to understanding the circle. Folding the circle in space extends our knowledge of traditional geometry by demonstrating a procedure for which there is no historical evidence. A step-by-step, hands-on method of folding and joining circles is presented. This modeling process generates patterns, develops forms and shows organization of systems that reflect our present understanding in all areas of spatial phenomena. More than an image, the circle is shown to be an in-formational tool, revealing a transformational process that extends our concept of the idea of Wholeness.

Wholemovement provides a mathematical classroom experience not possible in any other way. A comprehensive process of pattern formation is revealed through observation, inquiry, and direct, simple folding and joining circles. The patterns and forms developed are roots to mathematical, scientific and artistic understanding. There is an inherent order of patterning reflected in the movement of folding a circle, which provides a principled, universal view beyond human construction.

There is no age limit or educational requirement for folding a circle; it can be done by anyone who can fold a paper circle in half. Nine-inch diameter paper plates, 3/4-inch masking tape, a straight edge for creasing, and a few bobby pins are all the materials needed.

"The Seven Master Spirits of Paradise are the primary personalities of the Infinite Spirit. In this sevenfold creative act of self-duplication the Infinite Spirit exhausted the associative possibilities mathematically inherent in the factual existence of the three persons of Deity. Had it been possible to produce a larger number of Master Spirits, they would have been created, but there are just seven associative possibilities, and only seven, inherent in three Deities. And this explains why the universe is operative in seven grand divisions, and why the number seven is basically fundamental in its organization and administration"

The Urantia Book, Urantia Foundation, Chicago Ill. 1955

"Zero, it seemed, represented Absolute Reality. Infinity, or ∞, was the myriad manifestation of that Reality. Their mathematical product, $\infty \times 0$, was not one number, but all numbers, each of which corresponded to individual acts of creation."   Ramanujan

Robert Kanigel, "The Man Who Knew Infinity, the life of the genius Ramanujan"

"....mathematics must be approached as a whole."

"Spatial understandings are necessary for interpreting, understanding and appreciating our inherently geometric world."

NCTM Curriculum and Evaluation Standards for School Mathematics, 1989. The National Council for Teachers of Mathematics

"Nature is a unity in diversity... one great whole animated by the breath of life."
Naturalist, Alexander Von Humbolt

"Education is not merely acquiring knowledge, gathering and correlating facts; it is to see the significant of life as a whole."
"Any form of education that concerns itself with a part and not with the whole of man inevitably leads to increasing conflict and suffering."

Krishnamurti, "Education & the Significance of Life"

Contents

- 11 Preface
- 15 Introduction
- 21 In the classroom
- 25 Legend
- 27 Observations about folding, taping and joining circles.
- 31 Defining objects in space
- 33 The 5 Platonic Solids
- 34 The 13 Archimedian Semi-regular Solids
- 36 Proportional circle folding
- 39 Primary polygons
- 43 Grid development
- 44 Parallel grid
- 45 Systems
- 46 Number ten
- 49 Starting
- ● 51 The circle

57   **Folding Activities**   **Part 1**   Folding the circle into a 3-6 pattern

- ● 57   3FA-1   Folding the hexagon pattern
- ● 59   3FA-2   Reforming the hexagon pattern
- ● 61   3FA-3   Spherical Vector Equilibrium
-    62   3FA-4   Spherical matrix
- ● 65   3FA-5   Equilateral triangle
-    66   3FA-6   Down-folding the hexagon
-    67   3FA-7   Right angle tetrahedron puzzle
- ● 67   3FA-8   Tetrahedron
- ● 68   3FA-9   2-frequency tetrahedron
-    69   3FA-10   Pascal's Triangle
- ● 70   3FA-11   Octahedron
- ● 71   3FA-12   Octahedron in tetrahedron pattern
- ● 71   3FA-13   2-frequency octahedron
- ● 73   3FA-14   Triangle 4, 5, and 6
- ● 74   3FA-15   Tetrahedron star
- ● 74   3FA-16   Tetrahedron inside out
- ● 75   3FA-17   Tetrahedron inside out, 2-frequency
- ● 75   3FA-18   Tetrastar inside out
-    76   3FA-19   Tetrahelix
- ● 76   3FA-20   Transformational tetrahelix
- ● 77   3FA-21   Torus ring
-    78   3FA-22   2-frequency tetrahelix
-    79   3FA-23   Double helix
-    79   3FA-24   Octahelix

●   This mark shows basic getting started activities. Others can be introduced when appropriate.

- 80   3FA-25   Vector equilibrium/cuboctahedron
- 82   3FA-26   Four square tetrahedron
  82   3FA-27   Tetrahedron fractal
  84   3FA-28   Octahedron fractal
  85   3FA-29   Area of rectangle/triangle
  86   3FA-30   Tetratube transformation
  87   3FA-31   Tetratube development
  88   3FA-32   Octahedron movement system
  90   3FA-33   Variations on octahedron movement system
  91   3FA-34   Abbreviated octahedron movement system
  91   3FA-35   Irregular star
  92   3FA-36   Irregular octahedron movement system
  94   3FA-37   Reforming the tetrahedron
  98   3FA-38   Half moon tetrahedron

- **101   3FA-39   4-frequency diameter circle**

- 104   3FA-40   Hexagon disk
  105   3FA-41   Saddle hexagon
- 106   3FA-42   Pentagon cone
- 106   3FA-43   Bi-pentacap
- 106   3FA-44   Icosahedron
- 107   3FA-45   Convex dodecahedron
- 108   3FA-46   Concave dodecahedron
  109   3FA-47   Icosahedron/dodecahedron system
  110   3FA-48   Expanded dodecahedron
- 111   3FA-49   Stellated dodecahedron
  112   3FA-50   Extended tetrahedron
  114   3FA-51   Great stellated dodecahedron
  115   3FA-52   Extended tetrahedron variation
- 116   3FA-53   Small octahedron
  116   3FA-54   16-side deltahedron
  117   3FA-55   40 side triangular pattern
  120   3FA-56   Inside outside octahedron
  121   3FA-57   Octahedral spiral
  122   3FA-58   Winged octahedron
  122   3FA-59   Winged half octahedron
  123   3FA-60   Small rhombicoidodecahedron
  124   3FA-61   VE tetrahedron
  125   3FA-62   VE tetrahedron system
  126   3FA-63   Stellated octahedron
- 126   3FA-64   One half tetrahedron
  128   3FA-65   Four triangles form tetrahedron
  128   3FA-66   Four triangles form tetrastar
- 129   3FA-67   Tetrahedron/octahedron combination
  130   3FA-68   Six petal tetrahedron/octahedron
  131   3FA-69   Folded petal
  131   3FA-70   Truncated petals
  132   3FA-71   Equilateral triangle prism
  133   3FA-72   Right angle triangle prism
  135   3FA-73   Square prism
  135   3FA-74   Pentagon prism
  136   3FA-75   Anti-prism
- 137   3FA-76   Transformational anti-prism pattern
- 138   3FA-77   Octahedra in pentagon pattern

- **143 3FA-78   8-frequency diameter circle**

- 145 3FA-79   Truncated tetrahedron
  146 3FA-80   Variation of truncated tetrahedron
  147 3FA-81   Variations in tetrahedron pattern
  147 3FA-82   Variation in octahedron pattern
  148 3FA-83   Variation in icosahedron pattern
  148 3FA-84   Irregular truncated tetrahedron
  149 3FA-85   Joining truncated forms
  149 3FA-86   Footed triangle
  150 3FA-87   Footed triangle in hexagon pattern
  150 3FA-88   Footed triangle in spherical pattern
  151 3FA-89   Benzene ring matrix
- 152 3FA-90   Right angle tetrahedron
  154 3FA-91   2-frequency right angle tetrahedron
  154 3FA-92   Right angle octahedron
  154 3FA-93   Open right angle octahedron
- 154 3FA-94   Right angle tetrahedron cube
  155 3FA-95   Tetrahedral cube development
  156 3FA-96   Right angle tetrahedron-cuboctahedron
- 157 3FA-97   Transforming cube
  157 3FA-98   Transforming cube puzzle
  158 3FA-99   Irregular right angle octahedron
  159 3FA-100   Square tube
  159 3FA-101   Triangular tube
  160 3FA-102   Tetrahelix tube
  160 3FA-103   Octahelix tube
  161 3FA-104   Linear movement/non movement systems
  163 3FA-105   Hexagon 3, 4, 5
- 164 3FA-106   Dodecahedron/icosahedron
  165 3FA-107   3-frequency pentagon variations
  166 3FA-108   Bisection development of 8-frequency grid
  167 3FA-109   Folding Pi
- 169 3FA-110   Pythagorean Theorem

173   Folding Activities   Part 2   Folding the circle into a 4-8 pattern

- 173 4FA-1   Folding the square pattern
- 174 4FA-2   Spherical octahedron.
  175 4FA-3   Spherical octahedron variation
- 175 4FA-4   Triangle/square transformation

- **175 4FA-5   4-frequency diameter circle**

- 176 4FA-6   Small cube
  176 4FA-7   Variation on small cube
  176 4FA-8   Right angle octahedron
  177 4FA-9   Inside out stellated cube
  177 4FA-10   Octahedron cube combinations

- **178 4FA-11   4-frequency again**

- 178 4FA-12   Curved triangle
  179 4FA-13   Fractal movement
  180 4FA-14   Curved triangle again

- **181 4AF-15** **8-frequency diameter circle**

  182 4FA-16 Square faced vector equilibrium
  182 4FA-17 3/4 cube
  183 4FA-18 3/4 cube, vector equilibrium
  184 4FA-19 Transforming cube
- 185 4FA-20 Rhomicuboctahedron
  185 4FA-21 Rhomicuboctahedron sphere
  186 4FA-22 Cuberoot tetrahedron
  188 4FA-23 Cuberoot cube
  188 4FA-24 Double cube torus
  189 4FA-25 Cube/octahedron
- 190 4FA-26 Transforming octagon cross
  191 4FA-27 Variation in a cube

193 Folding Activities Part 3 Folding the circle into a 5-10 pattern

- 193 5FA-1   Folding the pentagon pattern
- 194 5FA-2   Icosadodecahedron sphere
  194 5FA-3   Expanded sphere
- 195 5FA-4   Short stellated icosahedron
  195 5FA-5   Long stellated icosahedron
  195 5FA-6   Long and short stellated icosahedron

- **197 5FA-7   3rd level pentagon development**

- 198 5FA-8   Dodecahedron solid
  198 5FA-9   Reconfiguration of pentagon
- 199 5FA-10 Cube/dodecahedron
- 200 5FA-11 rhombidodecahedron
  200 5FA-12 Variation in square pyramid
  201 5FA-13 Penrose titles

- **202 5FA-14 4th level pentagon development**

  203 5FA-15 Fractal development, 5-10
  204   Fractal development continued, 3-6
  205   Fractal development continued, 4-8

207 Documentation Part 4

  209 Photographs of models
  221 Selected bibliography
  223 About the author

Preface

It took Marcia Mikulac several months trying to convince me to join her in a geometry class taught by Hazel Archer back in 1979. Hazel had taught with Buckminster Fuller at Black Mountain College in North Carolina during the early fifties. The geometry she was teaching was not the abstracted, analytical geometry we get in school. It was Buckminster Fuller's geometry filtered through her own exploration and understanding.

My life had changed after three hours in that first geometry class with Hazel. I saw the world differently. The 2-dimensional and 3-dimensional forms we worked with were the same patterns. They were the same patterns of the geometry I had years ago in school, the same patterns inherent in all the art I had ever seen, and again the same in all the shapes and forms and systems I have seen others use to describe the universe. They are the same patterns observed everywhere in nature. If these patterns really are the organizational bases for all formation, why do we not teach them in school?

During that first class I made an assumption: *pattern was about the movement of universal formation and organization. It is observable, understandable and reproducible, and can be modeled by anyone.* Since that first class meeting, my days have been spent in pursuit of the correctness of that assumption.

The deeper I went into the geometry of spatial patterns the more connections were revealed. I tried to see how patterns form, where they come from and how they change. It took me into areas of research in which I previously had no interest. I spent long hours sorting through the conflicts between what I was observing and modeling, and what I had been taught. I had to draw and redraw to find the discrepancies.

When the models didn't work I had to find out if it was an error in perception or in procedure. Could I trust my perception, my skill, my ability to be consistent in the development of a given process? I spent many days trying to find and understand what lies behind the formulas for construction.

What I drew on paper I had to construct 3-dimensionally, making models in many materials and different forms. What I made models of I also had to draw. It was necessary to see if I really understood what I thought I did, in as many ways as possible. Soon I started to write about what I was drawing and modeling. The patterns revealed number relationships. The errors of inconsistancy made in one form were often caught in another. What seemed like a logical spatial development, when described in words would sometimes reveal inconsistencies that needed to be considered. I wanted to know how so many different configurations and functioning of things are formed in space. More importantly, I needed to know how things that are seemingly separated are all connected.

After five years of drawing, model making, writing and counting, I realized that these patterns also mirrored the development of my own life. I found new connections between diverse areas in my life, becoming more conscious of the movement between my inner being and my outer existence in space.

After years of trying to understand everything as an assembly of parts, I began to consider the idea of wholeness. The geometry was revealing a wholeness of process that was principled, ordered and inclusive to the evolution of endless parts. In understanding the sphere to be the only spatial form that inherently demonstrates the idea of wholeness, and the sphere compressed is a circle, I made my next assumptions: *the circle is whole, it contains everything.* If this is really so, how could I go about revealing some of that *everything*? How could that be true? Could I continue to cut the circle and work with fragments, if I understood the circle to be whole?

I went back to the way Buckminster Fuller used paper plates to demonstrate the pattern of the Vector Equilibrium, a 3-dimensional diagram of spherical order. Fuller would pass out paper plates to an audience and have them proportionally fold and join four circles into a complex patterned sphere. If the Vector Equilibrium could be made that simply by folding and joining four circles, I knew that everything else could be made from proportionally folding and joining circles.

I explored that idea with a class of fourth and fifth graders for a week. Folding circles engaged the children, providing an experience that generated ideas and concepts that traditionally were beyond their years. Through a simple process of folding a triangular grid into the circle, the children discovered that they could make many beautiful and complex forms. They felt good about themselves to be able to make things they never thought they could make, or could ever imagine. It was an exciting exploration. How much more was in a circle? How much more could be learned by folding paper plates?

Using only paper plates, I set out to reproduce ten years of geometric models, drawings and movement systems that I had made using traditional construction methods; toothpicks and glue, cardboard, wood, steel rods, ping pong balls, compass and straight edge. It all became so much easier and quicker folding the circle. There was no measurement, only the proportional movement of dividing into the circle. I could form a circle into a tetrahedron, truncated it, reform it into an octahedron, into a tetrahelix, transform it into a cube and a hundred other spatial configurations simply by an in-and-out moving of a pattern of folded lines. There appeared no end to the ways of forming and joining paper circles.

The more I folded, the more information that was unexpectedly generated. Mathematics was everywhere in the circle. It demonstrated a generalized foundation for arithmetic and the concepts behind fundamental mathematical theorems. I found proportional relationships of traditional construction methods of "plane" and "solid" geometry within the folding of the circle. This was not abstract information; it was an experience of in-my-hands, fold it and feel it mathematics.

The beauty of this is that all the forms are expressions in multiplicity of simple lines generated from the first division of the circle folded in half.

We need to rediscover the circle, maybe expand the definition of Geometry. We now have the experience of leaving this planet and going out into space. The circle is another spatial experience that needs to be explored.

The 'truth' of these revealed patterns and forms were actually modeling the concepts, theories, and ideas of mathematics; most of which I was only vaguely familiar. I found myself forming a philosophical, spiritual position directly from folding the circles. In observing the process of formation, developing complexities from where there was nothing but a single circle, I saw a spatial universe being created. I watched pattern and forms not there before develop into systems beyond what I could have imagined. The beauty was astonishing. Nothing was added or taken away. Why wasn't this common knowledge? How could it have been missed? The circle has always been around forever. We've had paper for many centuries. It is too simple? Am I naive? Have I rediscovered something others have found and discarded? Yet folding the circle was showing me a universe that was ordered, self-referential and exhibited principles that insured its growth and continual generation. I was watching a story of creation that can be duplicated by anyone who can fold a paper circle in half. I recreate that story every time I fold a circle. It is a simple story that helps me to find my place in the universe; a context of wholeness which gives meaning and value to my life.

Wholeness as a comprehensive idea is not evident in the conditions we have made for ourselves. The word has become an academic catchword. It is used to exclusively describe unified parts, to give importance to self-expressed ideas, rather than being used inclusively. Most of my life has been conditioned to belief in the importance of, and to delight in parts. The whole was conceptually too vast, too impersonal, too abstract, too remote, altogether too much to even think about. By folding circles I have found that unity belongs to the whole and not to the parts at all. We do not make a whole; it is simply a state of existence. Yet, I was continually putting parts together trying to form a unity, to make a whole, large enough to feel like I've done something important, and small enough that I still felt safe.

The whole of the circle offers a principled and clear direction that can be meaningful in our attempt to restore some balance to the unhealthy conditions we have created on this planet. I believe Wholemovement is a valuable approach that requires serious consideration. My hope is that there are teachers that will take this to their hearts and incorporate it into their classroom. It will make a difference in how children process information and direct their lives. I know relatively little about how to use the circle as a tool. But young children, if given the opportunity, will grow into knowing how to use it in ways that will allow them understanding that is not ours to have. At the very least they must have the option to know that the circle is every bit full as we think it is empty.

Bradford Hansen-Smith
Chicago, Illinois
September, 1999

INTRODUCTION

Geometry is no longer considered fundamental knowledge. It has become a subdivision of general mathematics. Over 2000 years ago in Greece it was thought of as a root discipline towards understanding. The study of geometry revealed the secrets of nature and the universe as a singular creation of God. It was a foundation for understanding natural sciences, the arts, architecture, music, mathematics, philosophy, religion, and the metaphysical nature of being. In different cultures at different times, the study of geometry has taken many forms, giving expression to a variety of interpretations. Through all cultural understanding runs a consistent patterned alphabet that is fundamental to formations found in nature. This pattern vocabulary is basic to the evolution of our understanding and knowledge about our universe.

This ageless vocabulary of spatial form consists of five regular polyhedra, called the Five Platonic Solids, and 13 Semi-regular polyhedra. They are primary to understanding Geometry and have everything to do with the formation of natural phenomena in our spatial environment. These patterns, even though traditionally they are called "solids", go beyond human invention and are fundamental to the organization of the universe. The study of these eighteen polyhedra fell from favor with the invention of non-Euclidean geometry about 150 years ago, a turning point in the development of mathematics. Geometry is no longer considered a major discipline. It has been taken apart and selected pieces absorbed into the main body of mathematics. Since then the study of Geometry has become the mechanics of human invention rather than the grand nature and subtle formation of universal expression.

There is no common familiarity with these principled geometric figures. We have forgotten their value. They are not taught in schools with any meaningful intentions. Instead, these polyhedra are treated as archeological artifacts, assumed to have little meaning in our world today. In upper grade levels, bits and pieces are used to support currently favored theories. Our obsession with parts, and tools for measurement has produced so much information that we have become overwhelmed and have lost connection to that which is principle. We are confused about what our children need to know because we are confused about what is important in our own lives. And yet, these spatial patterns keep reoccurring as we uncover more information in all areas of our lives.

We are familiar with circles that move; objects that roll on their edges, disks that rotate, concentric movement of circles. There are many things that are not circles, yet move in circular paths. The circle shape has a long history of practical applications. The image of the industrial age is a circular gear. The circle is an important tool. It is used for calculating and predicting, and regulating the workings of our lives. We have only begun to understand the circle as a container for storage and retrieval of information.

The circle patterns can easily be taught at the primary grade level. It is important to do so, but presently it is not considered with any priority at any grade level. Traditionally we think of the circle as a shape much like the square, triangle, and pentagon, differing only in that it has no angles. Using the compass to draw circles forms a biased understanding about the circle. We think about it from the center out. It is empty with nothing between the center point and the circumference. Our way of thinking about the circle has literally been shaped by the compass and straight edge, tools used by Euclid to put forth a system of proofs for "logical" thinking. His ideas have become the standard for mathematical and geometry construction, and to a large degree the day-to-day logic we use to process information. The static image of the circle is easily adaptable to abstraction conceptual development; and that is the way it has gone.

When the circle is considered as an object in space we are free to move and explore it in ways that are new and dynamic, revealing things not seen in the image of a circle. It is a way to know the circle by the movement of its wholeness, rather than by constructing images of parts. Folding the circle changes our understanding of the circle. It raises questions about many other things learn, that we have taken for granted.

Folding a paper plate into a tetrahedron and knowing it is at the same time an unbroken circle is a new idea. It is reformed into an octahedron, still the same circle with nothing added or taken away. That expands our thoughts about the circle a little more and adds to our understanding of the relationship between the octahedron and tetrahedron. While this may initially go against what we have been taught about constructing individual forms, it forces us to change our thinking about how we go about processing information. These and other transformations happen by making a few folds in a paper circle. Truths are revealed about principles, proportional forming and the organization of things in space that remain consistent no matter who folds the circle or how they interpret that information.

In exploring the movement of the circle there is a renewed sense of the mystery, beauty, and intelligence of Geometry that reflects so perfectly the patterns, forms, and intelligence observed throughout the universe. The circle shape is inherently whole; therefore making it cosmically relevant. It demonstrates a process that I call Wholemovement - the movement of the whole to itself.

This self-referencing movement of the circle generates a grid of ordered regular intervals that can be reconfigured into endlessly formations. These intervals of folded lines form a triangular matrix from which all primary spatial patterns can be modeled. As this grid is developed to higher frequencies it increasingly generates more information. Forms are developed from the movement of spacing within the pattern. The tetrahedron, or any reconfigured formation, always reflects the unity that is the circle. The circle is the context that effects the movement creating the grid matrix from which the circle can then be transformed and reformed.

Unity is not created by the tetrahedron or by combining forms in any specific arrangement. Unity is a principle quality of wholeness. Unity is not a temporal. No part or arrangement of parts can bring about unity. The circle demonstrates a process of unity moving to its own singularity, generating a patterned matrix that organizes and gives order to movement allowing ongoing development of parts within the circle.

There are seven qualities that I find in the first movement of the circle that are principle to all subsequent generative formation. In this regard, the circle implies far more than simply folding models of polygons, polyhedra, and spatial systems.

The circle is:

<u>Whole</u>
<u>Movement</u> in expression of the circle to the form of its own shape in
<u>Division</u> without separation, forming
<u>Duality</u> in symmetry with
<u>Triangulation</u> as pattern, having
<u>Consistency</u> of all parts individually, each with
<u>Dependency</u> to the whole.

These principles are inherent to the first fold of the circle. Development of subsequent folding that adhere to these principles will generate lines of divisional order forming in-out wave functions allowing for the entire surface to move in an organized unity of parts. The nature of each part is totally dependent on the whole; and that is what determines the interrelationships between individual parts.

There are many different perceptions of the value of the circle as it is patterned into this universe. There is no doubt about the importance of the circle in the human psyche, and the practicality of the circle in regulating and carrying out the rigors of human life. Our concept of the circle is conditioned primarily by mathematical usage as it has evolved from observations about the universe. Ancient cultures left images of circles, symbols of understanding carved and painted on rock walls, balls carved with circle patterns, huge circles formed using heavy stones, and large circles carved out of the earth. Our culture produces printed images of circles and machines, such as the computer, that draw circles. We make parts of circles out of every possible material, and form enormous circles of things that orbit the earth. These are all by-products from the quest of human consciousness towards understanding something about where we are.

Almost 2500 years ago, Thales of Miletus proved that the diameter divides a circle into two equal parts. While obvious to anyone, he demonstrated how to prove it using a self-referencing system of logic that could be abstractly communicated and understood by others. The circle has been the primary image used to develop and refine such generalizations and logic proofs that have led to the development of mathematics.

The circle continues to demonstrate itself to be our most useful and most comprehensive tool.

The circle disk is a compression of the sphere. Folding the circumference of the circle to itself forms a diameter that divides the circle in two equal parts. The proof is in the movement. The two folded parts are congruent, each fitting exactly to the other, in both directions. They form a spherical pattern of movement traced around the diameter. In the movement of the first fold of the circle lies the proof of its spherical nature. The sphere and the circle are two forms of the same singularity that inherently demonstrate wholeness. The image of the circle is a further abstraction of a compressed sphere.

There is a great amount of fundamental information about traditional Geometry in this first fold of the circle. One of the most important mathematical proofs is the Pythagorean Theorem; Proposition 47, Book I of Euclid's Elements. *"In right-angled triangles the square on the side subtending the right-angle is equal to the square on the sides counting the righ-angle."* Euclid's proof is sufficiently complex so that one needs an elaborate drawing to follow the step-by-step process of proof. Two folds of the circle give proof to the correctness and importance of that theorem about right-angle triangles (p. 169).

Anyone who has ever folded a circle in half has experienced that any two points on the circumference when touched together will fold the circle in half at right-angle to the direction of movement between the two points. That is the truth of what happens. It is from this first truth that all proofs of generalization can be made.

In a traditional Euclidean approach, generalizations about function are assumptions based on observations of many similar events. The events are isolated from context and given an image or symbol. The relationships necessary to substantiate the image must be constructed based on acceptance of imaged proofs about other events, enable to establish a closely connected logical sequence that will build a context to prove the initial assumption. All this is based on the acceptance of prior definitions of parts used in constructing static images. This is good exercise in a way of thinking, but proves nothing about the events themselves.

Since we rarely fold circles (and never for information) we don't pay attention to what takes place when they are folded. Folding circles is not part of our experience that has meaning. We use the circle for mechanical advantage, and as a symbol for nothing, a placeholder for something of value. Even the image gets cut up into pieces (arcs) for construction purposes. When used as a symbol for a whole, as in the degree mark, it denotes quantity of angle. The circle is used in many ways without considering the nature of the wholeness that it is.

Wholemovement offers an alternative approach to traditional Geometry without eliminating any understanding or previous information. Not only is the circle inclusive, it has a much higher out-put to in-put ratio, yielding far more information simply and directly than any other hands-on modeling system. To make a rough analogy, the circle is nature's compact disk. Within the generalization of its shape lies the pattern for individual formation encoded through proportional movement that reveals a process of specific information organization.

The diversity of forms and configurations that can be folded, and the combinations of systems that can be made by folding and joining circles is, for all practical purposes, endless. A diameter folded into the circle is without frequency. Three diameters folded into the circle divide each other in two equal parts making three 2-frequency diameters. At each level of folding, the division of the three diameters are again divided in half.

These folds form a triangular grid of an increasing number of intervals as each diameter doubles in frequency: 2, 4, 8, 16, 32... A nine-inch paper plate can easily be folded into a 16-frequency grid, even into a 32-frequency diameter grid and still be workable. By increasing the circle diameter, higher grid frequencies continue to be workable. The higher the frequency, the more points of intersection expanding the field of connections. This allows for greater combinations of points, lines and planes across a greater range of scale. Only up to the 8-frequency folded diameter grid is covered. Beyond this folded octave the same principles apply and the process continues forming greater complexity and more diverse systems.

The unresolvable difference between the distance around the circle and the distance of the perimeter of an inscribed hexagon is simply the difference between the whole circle and the diameter parts generated within the circle. The number difference is 3.1415... Pi. It represents three diameters (six points equal-distance on the circumference that form a hexagon) and the difference between the hexagon to the circle. This relationship of difference has no resolution. There is no equality between the whole and the created parts. The straight edge and compass are tools that separate the measure from what is measured. When a circle is folded, the straight line is never separate from the circle, nor is there confusion about what comes first or how the parts got there.

As the circle is continually folded new information is generated. The capability to recognize connections will increase and you will begin to recognize patterns that otherwise go unnoticed. I often think of the circle grid as a connection field in which the most unexpected things happen. As the circle is reconfigured through a large range of forms and systems, the unity of the circle is never broken; no parts ever left over. It is simply a pattern of unified movement that allows for changing formation through a touching of parts in its own wholeness. Everything that happens when forming the outside of the circle is an expression of inside movement.

The idea of Wholemovement is relevant and timely towards understanding the condition of our lives and how to go about making the changes necessary for health on this planet. It provides a universal standard beyond human construction by which we might evaluate our actions and bring them in line with that which is greater. There is no approach that is more principled, comprehensive, practical, or accessible to direct experience.

The activity of folding and joining circles can be understood by anyone who can fold a circle in half. It is especially important for young children to experience the wholeness of the circle, giving them a comprehensive context for all the individual parts that they will learn. It reveals a reflective, self-learning process having little to do with age, level of education, social or cultural condition.

While this approach has great benefit as a simple and direct hands-on activity and reveals much of the workings of Geometry and mathematics, it has profound implications to our understanding about the inexplicable nature of the wholeness of this universe.

In the classroom

This book can be used as a guide and resource to stimulate teachers and students in understanding the circle in a new way. It shows how the process of folding and joining circles allows students to generate geometric, mathematical information, and spatial designs of wonderful complexity. The potential lies in starting with understanding the idea of wholeness. The circle is whole in a way unlike any other shape or form. Some of the geometric forms will be familiar, many will not. The method of making them will be new. Do not be put off by the complex look of the drawings in this book. The density of compressed information on the flat page makes the drawings appear more confusing than the spread-outness of the 3-dimensional forms you will be folding. By folding a simple tetrahedron the circle is given a reality that a drawing can never do. The folding is easier than the drawings look. There is no measuring or formulas, only proportional folds of the circle to itself.

The activities are primarily a guide to the transformational process of the circle, while at the same time giving a good understanding for the fundamental patterns of traditional Geometry. Standard mathematics, beyond a few major theorems and formulas, is not presented. Math book information is inherent in the folded patterns and easily identifiable. The more you look the more you will find. Familiarity with folding and forming the circle, and with understanding the Five Platonic Solids as pattern will reveal far more than what is shown in this book.

The order of presentation is through a progression of movement that shows how patterns form and systems develop. Fundamental activities are indicated by dots in the table of contents. I would suggest they be done first. The comprehensive nature of the circle make it difficult to separate out specific activities by classification and logical connections of sequential development. Pick and choose those things that make sense or in which you see logical connections. Each activity is a direction of exploration that has it's own connections back into all of the other folding activities.

The images show the effects of the self-referenced movements of the circle. Tape and bobby pins are added to stabilize the forms. The actual movement of the circle from one "thing" into another and all the steps in between can only be experienced by folding the circle. This is not a read it and get it process. You must <u>do</u> the folding to have the experience to gain understanding.

In the section *Observations,* the mechanics of folding and taping is addressed. These are important; otherwise sloppiness can undermine the confidence of understanding. Problem solving on the mechanical level is part of the students' learning, as long as it doesn't frustrate and hinder the process. General information has been included, along with the classifications of basic polyhedron. Teachers should look at this information before beginning the folding. Students should fold first and be introduced to this information as it comes up in the folding. There is no reason to demonstrate how to make a tape hinge joint until there is a need to join pieces together in that way.

As forms are made, storage space will be necessary. Folded circle made while learning the process will be used later during more extended exploration. It is important to keep a number of models on display. Students often refer to previous models.

They observe differences and similarities, discovering deeper levels of pattern connections not obvious during the initial folding.

Joining inaccurately folded forms creates unnecessary problems. Initially, accuracy in folding is a function of paying attention. Close attention to consistency and accuracy in the beginning will eliminate problems later on. It is simply placing points together before creasing the folds. The more students fold the more accurate they become. The more accurate the forms, the easier they combine, the stronger they will be and the more beautiful they will look. This is learned best by folding circles and seeing what works and what does not work.

The *Starting* section presents a synthesis of approaches I have taken over ten years in the classroom. Beginning is a little different with each class. The information covered is consistent for all grade levels. This general approach helps get students into thinking comprehensively. It opens the mind to make connections otherwise unnoticed. The students look more closely, discovering new things about what is already familiar to them. Nothing is taken for granted. Students will organize information by experiencing a principled sequential process starting with the whole; dividing into it, continually generating information that is revealed one fold at a time.

The first class always starts with inquiry and exploration into the circle as an idea of wholeness. Familiar things are discussed in unfamiliar ways, always in the largest possible context. As we get deeper into the folding activity, students need to reflect less and work more. Some classes need the experience of working with their hands before they are ready to conceptualize. Inquiry is temporarily laid aside to be renewed later. Reflection on what they do, when ever it happens, is a critical part of the process.

Instructions are rarely given without demonstration. The first sequence of folds requires attention to what individual students are doing. Most students will quickly get a feel for the folding process; others must be shown individually.

Important words are underlined. A vocabulary emerges so we can talk together, with understanding, about what we are doing. As the book develops, I drop underlining words and ease up on the process of inquiry. It is the same in the classroom, the words become part of our conversation and inquiry becomes part of our on-going activity.

At first it is important to stop after each folding exercise to reflect on what we did and notice the new information. This helps establish an observant mind. It is principally from this information that we will know what follows, what to do next. After students reach a certain point of engagement in the folding process, it becomes more difficult to get them to regroup, reflect, and discuss what they have done. It is the same with teachers in workshop situations. This kind of involvement shows a need to engage concretely with substantive materials that work on many different levels. It enables us to process information differently.

Stopping periodically to come together for class reflection is also a way to stay connected with what everyone is doing. Much of group dynamics and social organization is modeled within the process itself. We start with individual work as a class, group in pairs, regroup in fours, return to individual work, then go to groups of eight and larger. Separation of tasks occur naturally according to the dynamic of the group. Groups mix as individual interest shifts. Often everyone is doing a different thing with the same folding process. When students see what others are doing, regrouping stimulates and develops new directions of exploration. The idea is to keep them moving towards developing a sense of individual value within the classroom experience. It is important to have students do projects and to present what they have done and their process of doing it to the class.

What I have suggested works well in most public school classroom situations. Even in extreme cases, students will find some degree of interest in the movement and transformational patterns of the circle. The patterns of movement are reflections of the same patterns that form our bodies and make up much of what is deep in our individual being. There is usually some level of resonance within most students.

Arrangement of Activities

The activities in this book are not arranged in a logical 1, 2, 3 sequence from "easy to hard." Following the general information section, the book is divided into three sections: the 3-6, 4-8 and 5-10 triangular grids; 3, 4, and 5 diameters respectively. Each section is further divided into increasing levels of diameter frequency development. Any kind of discrete classification would diminish the movement and transformative nature of the entire process. Once the basic grid folding is understood, it is easy to start with any number of basic folds and move into complex systems. There is the option to cover only simple forms, leaving the development of systems for further explorations. Or you might choose to move right into deeper levels of complexity, which will also clarify the process for other directions. An example of mix and match would be after folding the circle in half at the very beginning, you might want to introduce the Pythagorean Theorem as a function of the two right-angle relationships of a single folded diameter (3FA-110). Later when folding the tetrahedron, it will already be familiar as a pattern.

I have tried to show the amazing interrelatedness of diverse forms that can be generated from simply folding and joining circles. There are more activities in this book than any class will do. There are things your students will come up with that are not in this book. As teachers gain familiarity with the process, they will make their own connections and find the activities and ways that work best for them and their students.

In my experience most teachers will underestimate the level of interest, understanding, and patience that students bring to these activities. Often teachers are amazed at how quickly their students "get it" and the things they will do with it.

Problems usually occur when students get excited, rush to finish, lose the pattern, become inconsistent and don't finish all the folds necessary, or get lost in bad folds. This is the point when everything jams up and they get confused. The paper won't do what they want it to, so rather than taking time to feel the folds, discovering what the circle wants to do, they feel frustrated. Sometimes it just looks too difficult for them. They get most excited when they find out it wasn't. Because a child rarely has experience with using tape, things will sometimes fall apart and that may make them feel like they did something wrong. Young children sometimes have more trouble sticking tape than folding the circle. It is important to go over taping procedures with everyone learning the process, young and old.

A child's trouble with folding often has to do with not touching points together accurately. Once they understand that lines will always be in the right place when the points are touched accurately, they only have to concentrate on the points. When they get to that point the rest fall in line. Sometimes points get lost because the folds were not creased well. Some children have trouble identifying points on the edge of the circle.

These students, at first, only recognize the points of intersection on the inside of the circle. When students are in a hurry they forget some of the folds or do them sloppily. Too many creases, incomplete folding, or folds in the wrong place, get in the way of clearly seeing the grid pattern. If the lines get confusing and it becomes difficult to figure out what went wrong by looking at it, open the circle flat. By refolding the sequence of folds you should be able to find the problem. Everything that is done to the circle is recorded in the creased lines. Nothing is lost. What was not done is not there.

As you begin folding it is important to monitor everyone in the class for these potential problem areas, so they don't get in the way of the process. If folds become too inaccurate, it is better to start over with a "clean" plate.

Legend

For easy reference each **F**olding **A**ctivity is designated on the left hand side of the page preceding each activity. The first number (3, **4** and **5**) shows the number of diameters used for each grid. The number below the line is the number of the specific activity.

The curved black arrow means to fold in that direction over the top.

An outlined arrow means to fold under or behind. Sometimes you will see it pictured going under a shape.

The double arrow with the white arrowhead at one end means to turn over the piece being used.

The gray circle always represents the top side of paper circle facing up; folding over shows the bottom as white or light gray.

The white or gray lines on the circle show crease lines.

Sometimes folded lines will be black to emphasize certain aspects of pattern.

The dotted line shows which part of the circle that has just been moved

(3FA-24)   Curved brackets refer to related folding activities by section and number.

An underlined <u>word</u> usually means a word that may be important, not of common usage or needs to be specifically discussed.

bservations about folding, taping and joining circles

1. **Folding circles**

    There are two kinds of folding circles:

    a. **Touching two points together** generates a folded line perpendicular to the folding direction half-way between the 2 points. The relationship is dynamic.

    b. **Connecting two points** with a line folded through both is a static relationship.

    ☐ Two points touched together accurately will always put folded lines to the correct place.

    ☐ Be as accurate as you can; joining will be easier and the results better looking.

    ☐ Do not crease folds until you are sure the points are correctly placed. If a line is creased in the wrong place, it becomes confusing. It is then better to start over.

    ☐ Re-creasing on folded lines gives preference or memory to folding direction that is often helpful.

    ☐ Watch for creases lining up as points are folded together, that will indicate accuracy.

2. **Creasing the folds**

    ☐ Use a stiff, straight-edged object such as a ruler or wooden stick to make the creases.

     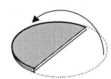 

    ☐ Crease the full length of each line to both ends on the circumference.

3. **Keeping track of folded lines**

    ☐ First trace folded lines with a pen or pencil. It makes seeing the patterns easier. To trace quickly and accurately, use the fold as a straight edge to guide your pencil.

     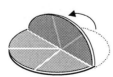 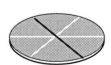

    ☐ Trace the edges of any polyhedra with a marker. When the circle is unfolded, you will have a map of it on the open circle grid.

4. Taping

☐ 3/4 inch masking tape works best for 9" paper plate size.

☐ Press tape really well onto paper for best hold.

☐ Put tape lengthwise (in long direction of edges) for a stronger and better looking joint. Taped edges will often reveal information about the pattern not otherwise obvious.

Two joined the same way.

☐ Put 1/2 length of tape on one edge to be joined and place the other edge next to it in position and fold the tape over onto the joining piece.

☐ When taping end points together, tape as shown below on edges across the joining points so that it covers both adjacent planes that come to the point of connection. Squeeze the tape together at the joining.

☐ Make a <u>hinge joint</u> by joining 2 polyhedra on their edges so they move.
    a. Put the edges of the 2 objects together; rotate them around the edge axis until they go no further. Then put 1/2 of tape on each side of the length of pieces to be joined.
    b. Rotate on the edge axis all the way around to the other side as far as it will go and put a piece of tape down the axis length as on the other side. This gives a full of range of motion to an edge-to-edge hinge joint.

a.   b.

The taping method pictured above is the simplest, cleanest looking, as well as the strongest way to tape a reflective movement joint.

☐ When making a cone, fold 2 or more sections of the circle to the inside. Tape the folded flap to the inside surface to keep it from getting in the way of other folds.

← tape flap across edges

☐ Tape will eventually dry out and fall off. For more permanent joining, put white glue on joining surfaces and apply tape to hold the pieces in place. Remove tape after glue is dry.

5. Cutting

☐ <u>Never cut the circle</u>. Sometimes a student will not fold evenly and will trim the uneven edges to make it look neat. We always open it out flat to see that it is now less when a part is cut off. It is no longer whole. Comprehensive thinking means no short <u>cuts</u>, literally. When taking short cuts things always get lost. No cutting circles.

☐ There are interesting designs and many kinds of complex systems that can be made by cutting into the circle. Cutting slits around corner points to open them for joining together is occasionally necessary, but that is secondary to understanding the principles and working with the wholeness of the circle. *The circle is not cut into parts.*

6. Materials

☐ Uncoated 9-inch <u>paper plates</u> work best and are the cheapest. They are a good size for most students. Any large grocery or discount stores will carry *lightweight, uncoated inexpensive* paper plates. Circles of any size can be cut out of many kinds of foldable paper. I encourage students to explore that direction as well.

☐ I use 3/4-inch <u>masking tape</u>. Cheaper tapes have more stickiness; that is good.

☐ Standard size <u>bobby pins</u> usually come on a card of 60 at any drug store.

☐ Any kind of sturdy <u>straight edge</u> or ruler will work for creasing the folds. For my classes I use paint stirring sticks cut into half-lengths.

☐ White glues are okay, Elmers Carpenter Wood Glue works best. It dries quickly and will not dissolve when using water base paints over it. Models will last longer when applying glue before taping. Remove tape when glue is dry.

Defining objects in space

There are 3 primary ways of describing, viewing, joining, and moving 3-dimensional objects in space: by end <u>points</u>, by edge <u>lines</u>, and by surface <u>planes</u>.

1. Three parts that describe an object

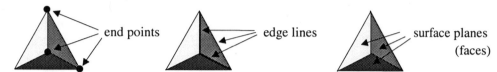

2. Three symmetries from which to view an object

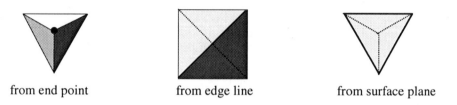

from end point   from edge line   from surface plane

3. Three ways objects can touch

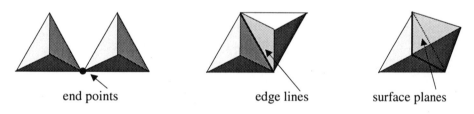

end points   edge lines   surface planes

4. Three kinds of movement of objects

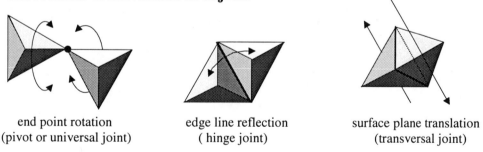

end point rotation   edge line reflection   surface plane translation
(pivot or universal joint)   (hinge joint)   (transversal joint)

    The circle is a <u>point</u> location with a boundary <u>line</u> of definition that describes a <u>plane</u>. A circle has no inherent scale; it is concentric, that is centered to itself. The circle is whole; showing point, line, and plane, without separation. Straight lines are proportional measures of division within the circle.

The 5 Platonic Solids

Patterns of spatial organization

tetrahedron

4 end points
4 sides
6 edges

octahedron

6 end points
8 sides
12 edges

cube

8 end points
6 sides
12 edges

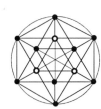

icosahedron

12 end points
20 sides
30 edges

dodecahedron

20 end points
12 sides
30 edges

There are only 5 spatial patterns that exhibit a regularity of faces, edge lengths, corner angles, and edge angles of adjacent faces. Traditionally they are called the 5 Platonic Solids, or the 5 regular polyhedra. Usually perceived individually and studied separately as volumetric solids, these 5 polyhedra exist as individualized aspects of a singular spherical pattern.

The tetrahedron, octahedron, and cube patterns are inherent in the closest packed order of spheres of the same size. The icosahedron and dodecahedron are another level of spherical order showing a shifting of position of spheres.

The interconnections observed of these polyhedra push the boundaries of our logical separation and abstract systems of classification. They exhibit a consistency of inner relationships difficult to explain, deeply rich, yet easily modeled and demonstrated within the context of the singular nature of the circle.

The fundamental shapes in the 5 polyhedra are the triangle, square, and pentagon -the 3, 4, and 5. Three are of triangles, one is of squares and one is of pentagons. These patterns appear everywhere in nature and are equivalent to a spatial alphabet. They are the 5 patterned elements fundamental to development of life systems in this spatial universe.

The transformational nature of each polyhedron is apparent in the corresponding numbers of end points, edge lines and surface planes. The numbers show 2 sets of dual forms. The tetrahedron is considered without a dual. Within spherical order the tetrahedron and octahedron are 2 parts of the same pattern.

This image holds the information for all 5 platonic solids. All points fall within the hexagon division of spherical order.

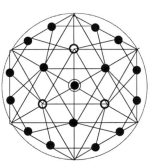

The 13 Archimedian Semi-regular Polyhedra

The Five Platonic Solids are letters, the alphabet of spatial formation, and the 5 single most primitive forms of spatial organization. They exhibit 3 primary shapes: the equilateral triangle, the square, and the regular pentagon.

This alphabet of spatial formation has 5 patterns of regular composition, and the next level has 13 consonants of semi-regular composition: 18 separate spatial components from which endless design of spatial expression can be generated.

The 13 semi-regular polyhedra are called the <u>Archimedian Solids</u>. Traditionally they are classified by systematically cutting away the corners from the 5 primary polyhedra. Since all 13 semi-regular seem to be derived from the 5, they can be understood as basic subsets of spatial formation. The division of the 3, 4 and 5 generate 6, 8, and 10. This increase in number of sides of polygons as they are found in these semi-regular polyhedra is consistent in the three proportional forming of the 1:2 ratio of the circle, 3-6, 4-8, and 5-10 (p. 36).

Of the 13 semi-regular polyhedra, the Vector Equilibrium, traditionally called the cuboctahedron, is in fact spherical pattern of order. It is the pattern of 12 spheres all touching the center sphere; a centered system of 13. It is fundamental order, primary to all other 12 polyhedra.

The Vector Equilibrium is the truncated semi-regular of both the cube and the octahedron. The octahedron is a truncation of the tetrahedron, both regular polyhedra. The interconnection of spherical order between these formed patterns defies the strictness of this system of classification based on outward appearances.

The icosadodecahedron is another of the semi-regular polyhedra that is fundamental spherical pattern of both the icosahedron and dodecahedron combined. These 2 forms separately are 2 of the 5 regular polyhedra. Together they are the full expression of 12 spheres in a non-center order having shifted to a 5-fold symmetry.

The Platonic and Archimedian Solids are important to understanding pattern development of spherical order which can all be demonstrated by folding and joining circles.

These are images of solid representation of the 13 semi-regular polyhedra. They are made from combinations of triangles/ hexagons, squares/octagons, pentagons/decagons; all reflecting the 1:2 ratio of primary division.

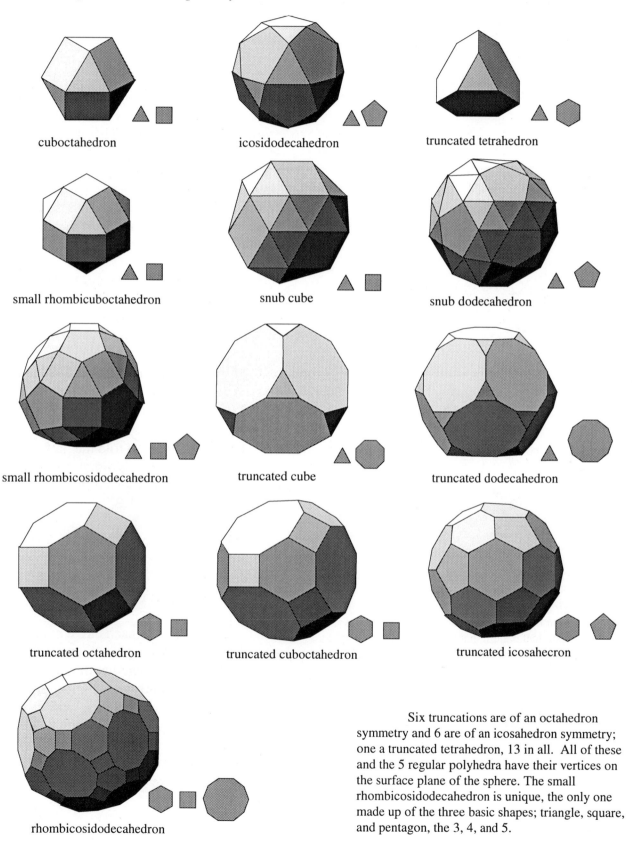

cuboctahedron

icosidodecahedron

truncated tetrahedron

small rhombicuboctahedron

snub cube

snub dodecahedron

small rhombicosidodecahedron

truncated cube

truncated dodecahedron

truncated octahedron

truncated cuboctahedron

truncated icosahecron

rhombicosidodecahedron

Six truncations are of an octahedron symmetry and 6 are of an icosahedron symmetry; one a truncated tetrahedron, 13 in all. All of these and the 5 regular polyhedra have their vertices on the surface plane of the sphere. The small rhombicosidodecahedron is unique, the only one made up of the three basic shapes; triangle, square, and pentagon, the 3, 4, and 5.

Proportional folding

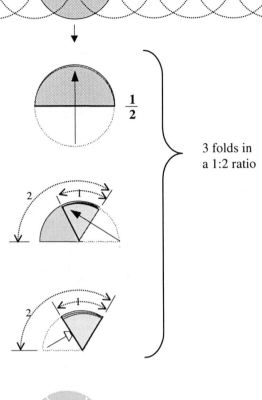

3 folds in a 1:2 ratio

3/6

Diameter folded in half.

Four circles join into a spherical pattern that shows 4 great circles.

13 points

There is only one way to fold the circumference of a circle so that it will touch itself completely. That is to fold it in half. From this self-referenced circle movement a proportion of 1:2 is generated, one whole in two parts. The circle has been reformed. All subsequent movement and reformation of the circle comes from this 1:2 triangulation.

There are only 3 ways to again fold the circle (already folded in half) and remain consistence to the first movement of proportional division.

- The first generates 3 diameters and 6 equal divisions, a 3-6 division folded 3 times proportionally 1:2.

- The second way to fold the half folded circle reveals 4 diameters and 8 divisions, a 4-8 division. It is folded 4 times to the ratio 1:2.

- The third way to fold the half-folded circle shows 5 diameters and 10 divisions in a 5-10 pattern. It is folded 5 times proportionally 1:2.

The diameters of each circle develop different edge lengths. When each circle is folded together they will reform differently. Each joined in multiples, in triangulation, will form spheres of equally spaced great circles of 4, 3, and 6 respectively. The form of 3 great circles in the sphere of the 4-8 folding are 4 folded circles.

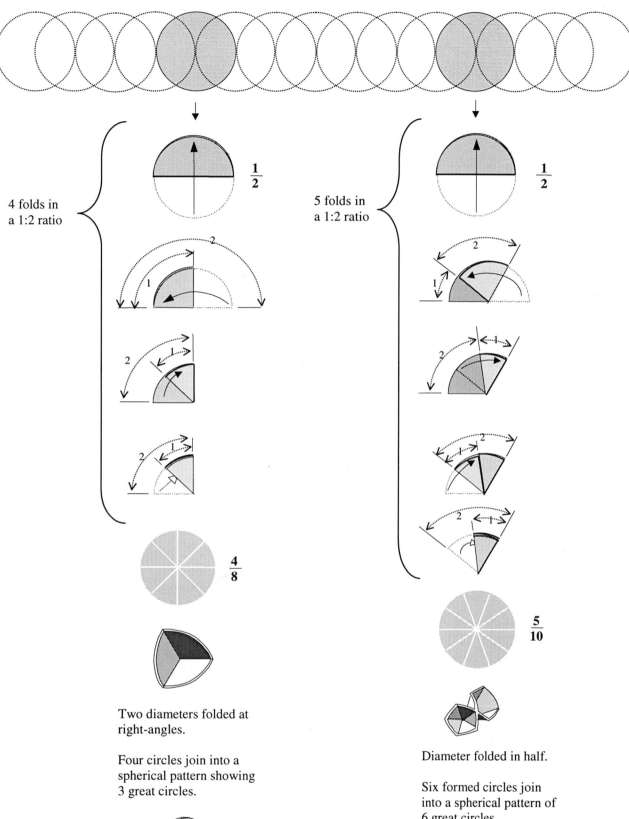

4 folds in a 1:2 ratio

5 folds in a 1:2 ratio

Two diameters folded at right-angles.

Four circles join into a spherical pattern showing 3 great circles.

7 points

Diameter folded in half.

Six formed circles join into a spherical pattern of 6 great circles.

31 points

Primary polygons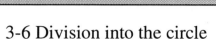

3-6 Division into the circle

HEXAGON

The hexagon is 3 diameters through the center, all equidistant around the perimeter. This pattern division of 13, 7 points and 6 intervals, is the first formed measure of the circle to itself. The hexagon shape is implied, but unformed. The hexagon, pentagon, square, and triangle are all functions of the hexagon pattern division of the circle.

Fold over 6 times around to form the hexagon shape.

To fold the hexagon shape, fold between each of the 6 points on the circumference. Cutting the circle to make the shape would reduce the whole to a part, limit the function to that shape and create waste. In folding the circle, it remains whole, and can be transformed to other shapes and reconfigured with nothing left over.

The right-angle movement of the first division into the circle is what determines proportional congruency, or unity between folded parts. The hexagon is a 2-frequency development of each diameter. Opposite edges of the hexagon shape parallel the diameters making the hexagon a consequences of intersections. The lines of division are generated by the movement of the circle to itself. The primary relationship of parts (straight lines) to whole (circle) is reflected in the importance of the number 3.1415..., Pi. The first level of grid development of the hexagon pattern is the 4-frequency diameter grid. Each of the 3 diameters is divided equally into 4 sections.

   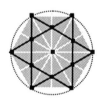

This 4-frequency grid is the result of folding a right-angle relationship of each of the outside 6 points to the center point and each end point of the diameter to the opposite. It is the full-formed expression of the 7-point hexagon pattern, the same as if you were to draw a line from each of the 7 points to all the others. The circle is divided into 12 equal sections, with 6 diameters. This shows the first formed hexagon shape to be the center to a hexagon star. It forms within the grid pattern, not on the circumference. This 4-frequency development corresponds to spherical order and likewise everything is derived from this basic pattern matrix. The hexagon pattern reveals information for all subsequent polygons, and polyhedra.

TRIANGLE

Fold in 6/12 (1/2) (3/6) of the circle, folding 2 halves of the diameter edge together. This forms a 6-sided cone with an open hexagonal interval. The curved sides can easily be folded between the 3 star points making it tetrahedron. Notice the stability of the triangle interval compared to the 4 and 5 shaped intervals.

Folding the circumference over on either of the inscribed triangles forms a flat triangle with a tremendous amount of divisional information.

5-10 Division into the circle

The 5-10 division of the circle is a function of the same folding pattern as the hexagon; the difference is in the proportional division of the 1:2 ratio. Five diameters are generated in a decagon division. Here the pentagon is of a flat division of the circle rather than 3-dimensional. There are 2 opposing pentagon shapes inherent to the 10 fold as there are triangles to the hexagon pattern and hexagons to the 12 division.

Fold the circumference under between each point for the decagon shape. Do the same between alternate points for the pentagon. Fold the diagonals of the pentagon to form the star.

Fold in 1/5 of the circumference of the pentagon shape forming a square base pyramid.

Fold in 2/5 of the circumference of the pentagon shape forming a triangular pyramid, a tetrahedron.

PENTAGON

Fold in 2/12 (1/6) of the 2-frequency circle. This leaves 5/6 of the circle in a decagon pattern. The hexagon star has been reformed into a pentagon star, 5 diameters. The flat hexagon has gone into a 10-sided open-base cone. The pentagon is now more than just a flat shape. The folds between the star points form the pentagon cone shape into a pentagonal pyramid. The 6/12 grid has reconfigured into the form of a 5-10 grid while remaining 6/12 in pattern, recoverable through a single movement.

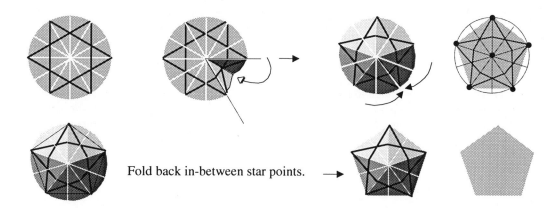

Fold back in-between star points.

Notice how little information there is with the flat pentagon shape. By reducing it to a simple shape removed from the dynamics of the circle, it has little meaning with minimum information. All flat shapes are compression of spatial information usually in the form of a simplified image where all the good contextual stuff has been eliminated. All polygons are multi-functional parts within spatial systems and should be learned in that way, rather than isolated parts without any context.

SQUARE

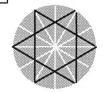 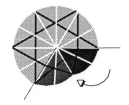 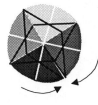 

Fold in 4/12 (2/6) (1/3) of the circle on the center point between 2 points on the hexagon star. The hexagon star transforms into a square star. Fold the circumference flap between the 4 points to form a square, open-based pyramid. The square and the pentagon shapes have no stability unless held rigid on a flat surface. Notice how the angle of the pyramid has changed as the number of sides decreased and the height increase.

4-8 Division into the circle

The circle folded into the 4-8 division, in the same way as with the 5-10 and 3-6 pattern, will generate information through the same process of development. Both the octagon and the square shape can be formed by folding between every point and between every other point. As with the hexagon and the pentagon, there is a duality of shape to each pattern.

   Fold circumference between alternate octagon star points to the back forming one of the 2 squares.

By folding the 4 corners of the square to the center point forming a smaller square making a 2-frequency diameter grid.   Again, there is very little information with just the outside shape of the square.

 Fold in from the center point 2/8 (1/4) of circumference. This forms a right-angle tetrahedron.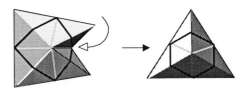

This diagram shows the circle divided from which are generated the <u>six</u>, <u>five</u>, <u>four</u>, and <u>three</u> sided polygons, all from right-angle movement. I have included the line as a plane that has 2 sides and the circle as reduction of the line to a single plane, a point. It is easy to see the process of division of the circle into individual folded forms and the common shapes within. Each folded form is the <u>two</u> sided circle plane that remains <u>singular</u>. The circle is where we start and where we end, with a lot of movement in-between. Each pattern of any given frequency can always be folded down into each of the primary components of the circle. This process is not unlike factoring.

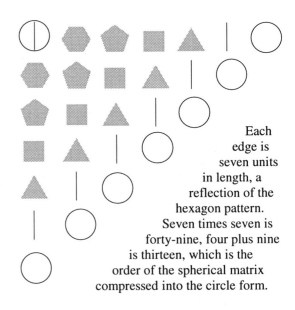

Each edge is seven units in length, a reflection of the hexagon pattern. Seven times seven is forty-nine, four plus nine is thirteen, which is the order of the spherical matrix compressed into the circle form.

Grid development

The only movement constant with the circle shape is the self-referencing movement of the circumference. This generates a diameter. The information of one whole to 2 parts is a 1:2 ratio that is directive to continuing to fold the circle to itself. That happens in 3 ways, each a different proportion of circumference division that determines how many 2-frequency diameters will divide the circle.

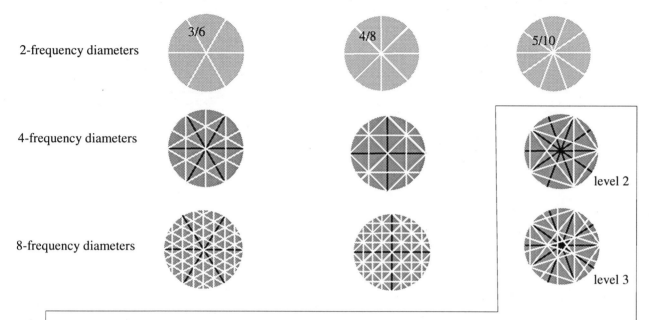

Because of the different proportional divisions of the five-fold symmetry from the 3-6 and 4-8, the term "frequency" is not appropriate, I use "level" to differentiate between the different size of pentagons generated at different levels of consistence development.

The 2 columns show folding the circle into 3 triangular grid patterns, the <u>equilateral triangle/hexagon</u>, the <u>right-angle triangle/square</u>, and the <u>golden ratio triangle/pentagon</u>. Each step generates new points of intersection along the diameter lines. It is this patterned information that is necessary to generate a higher frequency grid.

The nature of the circle as pattern is that all circles are the same. These 3 foldings can then be seen as one sequential function of the movement of a circle. That function reveals an initial growth pattern called the <u>Fibonacci series</u>. The sequence of numbers shows that the proportion of one part to the second part is the same proportion as that of the second part to the sum of parts one and 2. The three 1:2 division of the circle reflect the beginning of this sequence. All the foldings in this book are expressions of "one" circle in self-reflected multiple movement.

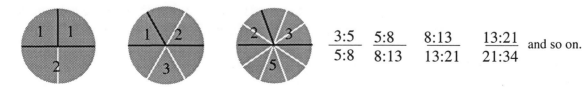

Parallel Grids

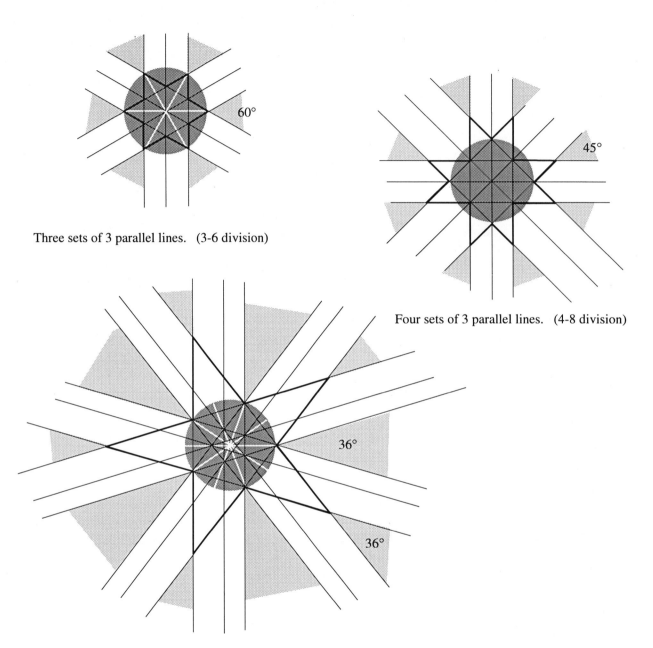

Three sets of 3 parallel lines. (3-6 division)

Four sets of 3 parallel lines. (4-8 division)

Five sets of 3 parallel lines. (5-10 division)

      Each of these expressions shows directional crossings with sets of 3 lines in parallel. The hierarchy of pattern is established in spherical order and finds expression in the hexagon pattern of the circle. This pattern is 3. It reveals the symmetry of 3 sets of 3 lines each, (3 x 3 = 9) plus 3 diameters (9 + 3 = 12), and (1 + 2 = 3). This reflects the nature of 3. The 4-8 division is 4 to the nature of 3. The 5-10 grid is 5 to the nature of 3. (3 + 4 + 5 = 12). 12 is reflected order of the nature of 3. The circumference generates a single diameter that increases to 3, 4 and 5, expanding outward, observed in the star formations.

Systems

Three primary classifications of spatial systems can be identifiable as ways that individual forms fit together: point, line and plane. It all starts with the form of the sphere, which is the point. The first movement of the circle towards individualization of parts is a boundary line that shows planer division with corner points of angulation. These are a result of a single movement. They are separate only in the human mind.

All forms represented in this book are circles and straight lines. Every visual image and symbol is fundamentally created from circles and straight lines. Each of these letters are circles and straight lines. That is all there is; endless parts of circles and straight lines and all the different ways they combine and recombine to generate diverse systems of information.

A system is the coordinated movement of individual parts towards a specific function. Parts of different systems are interchangeable and they function in many systems simultaneously. All systems are interrelated sharing the same order of spherical pattern having developed through cosmic evolution to inconceivable levels of complexity. A unity of parts grouped to common purpose is usually identified as a system. Any individual forming is always a system. Primary spherical system is the tetrahedron, 10 points in space. The first fold of the circle shows that 4 points are minimum tetrahedral expression. The circle, line, and plane systems are each partial reflections of spherical movement.

The 5 regular polyhedra are important patterns for the formation of individual systems. Being parts of the same order there is total interrelationship between all evolved formations. The point, line, and plane are parts of systems that are themselves formed into spherical, linear, and planer systems, observed to be of the same pattern no matter how irregular the forms appear. Somewhere in there must be included the spiral and the helix. They are directional parts of spherical movement and are observed on all levels of formations.

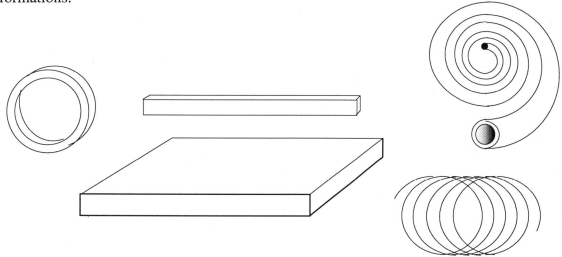

Number Ten

Circle

 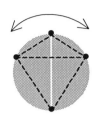

The first fold of the circle reveals the number 10. Touching any 2 points on the circle together generates 2 more points that create 6 edge relationships in space. This is the tetrahedron; 4 corner points plus the 6 edges is a pattern of 10. The tetrahedron is the first spatial pattern of division by folding the circle (p. 54).

The primary relationship of the circle to its full measure is the hexagon, a pattern of 3 diameters. There are 6 points on the circumference and the center point makes 7. The 7 points of intersection plus the 3 individual diameters together are the number 10. Seven is inherently the principle expression of the circle proportionally to itself 3 times and 10 is the total generation of organizational components.

From within O comes 3. From 3 is generated 7 inherent in the pattern of 10.

Sphere

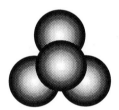 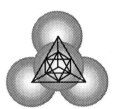

10 is reflected in the number of spatial locations of a single sphere reformed into in a tetrahedron pattern of 4 spheres: 4 spherical locations plus 6 points of connections is 10 specific locations in space. Ten is the first singular divisional pattern expression of the sphere.

Dual circle

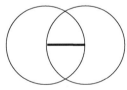 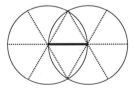

10 is reflected in the points of intersection of the dual circle. One radius is 2 end points that are reciprocal inside/outside forming the image of 2 intersecting circles. 4 points when connected along diameters reveal 10 points of intersection.

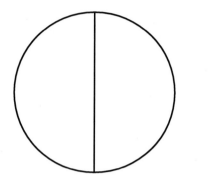

division

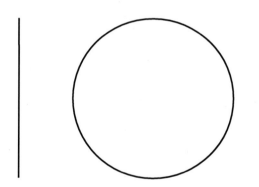

separation

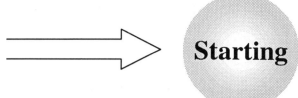

Starting

Where do we start?
From where we are right now.

Where are we?
This question is discussed by the class, considering different ideas of individual location: in a chair, the classroom, school, city, country, etc. Location is expanded to include all of space, as far as can be imagined. We are *all* in *all* of space. We forget that space has no parts. It has no discernable beginning or end. It is endlessly whole. Space appears to be in the form of a <u>sphere,</u> expanding, evolving. *Discussion might follow with observations about a sphere: continuous surface, no beginning or end, the same everywhere, without scale, complete, no part; even how astronomers can tell from the inside what the "outside" shape looks like.* We are inside of a single spherical ball of existence, a space/time expanding universe. We all are places individually occupied within this singular <u>whole</u> ball of movement. As parts of the universe we are totally <u>dependent</u> upon the universe for our individualized existence, and that determines how we <u>interrelate</u> to each other and to all the other parts. This often initiates a discussion about wholeness and how we find out about what it is.

How did we get here?
We came into this immensely large spherical universe through the development of a very small single spherical egg cell. This spherical cell, like a ball, is whole. This singularity <u>divides</u> and <u>multiplies</u> into a <u>duality</u> that looks like two of the same, though still connected as one in the form of two. Wholeness can only generate the whole of what it is, even in dual form, which then generates a double duality. Two whole balls divide into 4 whole balls. The 4 balls are still singular and whole with all still connected to each other without separation.

This growth can be demonstrated using one tennis ball, then adding another. Have 2 balls touching, then 2 sets of 2 balls joined at right-angles to each other, with all 4 balls touching each other. This forms a 3-sided pyramid forming an open space in the middle of the 4 balls. *Another demonstration, though more difficult, is to squeeze and twist a half-inflated balloon around the middle forming the appearance of 2 balloons. Squeeze at right-angle to the first squeeze, around the middles of both spherical forms and twist. What is one balloon, a single surface, now looks like 4 all connected through the center space.*

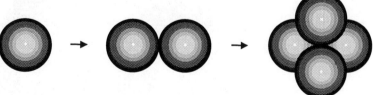

Another way to demonstrate the same pattern is to touch your index finger to your thumb. Do this with both hands and put the 2 fingers and 2 thumbs all touching each other forming a double duality. If it looks like a square, they are not all touching each other. Turn the 2 sets of 2 at righ- angle to each other as in the movement of the children's rhyme, "itsy-bitsy-spider went up the water spout."

One sphere multiplied times itself is 2. Two times itself again is 4, still singular and whole. This is more than adding up separate balls, it reflects cell generation starting from a single cell. It is multiplication through division without separation. The next in the series would be 4 to itself becoming 8. To do this a change must occur; singularity is broken, 2 balls must separate opening the space for growth and further development.

It is often appropriate at this time to talk about the 4 spheres and the 6 <u>tangent points</u>, the connections where they touch. It is a pattern of 10 specific locations or points in space. It is called a <u>tetrahedron pattern</u>, when in fact it is both the <u>tetrahedron</u> and <u>octahedron</u> simultaneously. Each sphere is nestled into the space formed by the other 3 spheres. That makes all 4 spheres triangular in pattern forming a relationship of 3 individual squares where the 4 spheres are connected (p. 70) This arrangement can extend infinitely. It is called the "closest packing, most stable order of spheres that are the same size". This preexistent order is the matrix in which all geometric patterns can be found.

one sphere

four spheres

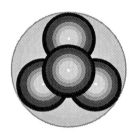

twenty spheres
(five sets of four)

the Circle

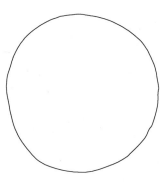

Often I start by drawing a circle on the chalkboard. I ask the students to explain what it is. This indicates the level they are thinking on. Usually they say a circle. I draw a picture of a tree or dog and ask them what it is. When someone says it's a picture of the object then we can talk about the circle as a picture, an image that represents a circle. We then discuss what a circle is. Many things are in the shape of a circle. The circle is a shape in space. It moves. It is <u>dynamic</u>. The image of the circle is <u>static</u>. To find out something about a thing, we go to the thing directly. The big difference is that things in space move, images of things do not. Images that appear to move are sequentially constructed images.

It is instructive to draw a circle freehand, do it with a compass, or trace around a circular object on a piece of paper. What information can be generated from that circle image without adding anything to it? The circle is only whole if nothing can be added to it or taken away. When we add lines and points to the drawn circle it has diminished to a part in the shape of a circle. Cut the circle out with a pair of scissors and observe the difference between the drawn image and the circle in space.

Observe the sphere; from every view it looks the same. That look is the shape of the <u>circle</u>. The sphere compressed, or flatten into a single plane would be a circle in space with 2 surfaces. Any slice through a sphere is in the shape of a circle, but then the wholeness of the sphere would be lost.

To explore the circle in space we will use paper plate circles. Moving the circle in space is about wholemovement, movement of the wholeness of the circle to itself. Nothing is added or taken away. There are only the effects of self-referenced movement.

By describing the circle, a lot of information can be revealed. It has a front and back, 2 surface <u>planes</u>, and a continuous edge <u>line</u> called the <u>circumference</u>. Sometimes we talk about the edge line having 2 corners where the edge plane and the 2 surface planes come together forming a defined space having volume. The circle in space is a <u>disk.</u>

The circle has no <u>scale</u>. Up close it is a circle, at a distance, a point. A circle can be a borderline, or a solid plane. It can be empty, with nothing, or full with everything. The <u>concentric</u> nature of the circle is evident in the spinning and rolling around its <u>center</u>. We talk about the circle in space as a point location, having line, plane and volume. The circle is its own center, showing <u>duality</u> and <u>symmetry</u> of parts.

Primary to the circle in space is that it has a *circumference* definition and *moves*.

Folding the circumference

Each student gets a paper plate and a wooden straight edge to crease the folds. *We move the circumference so that it touches itself.* When asked to fold the circle in half, we usually do not think about what we do, nor do we pay attention to the information that is generated. There are 2 ways to approach folding the circle in half. Sometimes we do it both ways.

ONE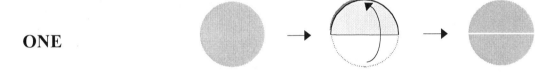

Put the circumference exactly on to itself. Crease with the wooden straight edge. The circle is folded in half. This is a <u>self-referenced</u> movement. Observing myself and others folding circles, I've learned we all do the same thing by putting 2 imagined points on the circumference together, then looking to see if the rest of the edge is lined up. *Any 2 points on the circumference when touched together will exactly fold the circle in half.* Knowing this makes it easier to fold the circle accurately.

What new information do we have that was not there before the circle was folded?

The circle now has a line. This line is called a <u>diameter</u>; it divides the circle in 2 equal parts. The circle parts are <u>congruent</u> because one part fits exactly onto the other, being the same size and the same shape. With the circle open, the 2 congruent shapes are <u>symmetrical</u>. The diameter is the <u>line of symmetry</u> between the 2 parts. This kind of <u>balance</u> shows a pairing of one right-handed part and one left-handed part. When the circle is folded, both parts are in the same <u>orientation</u>. With 2 parts we can talk about the relationship of 1 whole to 2 parts, called a <u>ratio,</u> 1:2. There is another relationship of one part out of a total of 2 parts, called a <u>fraction</u>, 1/2, also 2/2, two of two parts. The shape of the circle folded shows us a <u>straight-line</u> edge, 2 <u>curved</u> edges and 2 <u>corner points</u>.

The 2 corner points are <u>points of intersection</u> where the diameter meets the circumference. When the circle is moved from open to closed, there is a changing <u>angle</u> between the 2 congruent planes. The movement of folding goes in both directions, opening and closing, to the front and to the back. The front and back are <u>reciprocal</u> as inside and outside. The diameter is the center <u>axis</u> around which the 2 parts revolve, tracing the pattern of a sphere in space. The compressed sphere moving around its diameter reflects back it's spherical nature.

All this information need not be talked about at this point, particularly if the attention is focused on the folding activities. I suggest key words, from those underlined, be used in talking about the folding activities so students become familiar with them. Words determine how we understand the specific parts, functions, and relationships we observe. To accurately describe specific functions makes it easier to talk about the folding activities. It is fascinating that there is so much information in simply folding a circle in half.

TWO

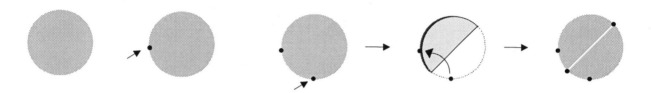

Make one point anywhere on the circumference. Mark another point anywhere on the circumference. There is a relationship between the 2 points. Usually we draw a line from one point to the other to show the relationship between them. Nothing has been generated; it only makes visible a relationship of distance already there. We discuss relationship. *Relationships are about touching.* The expression of any relationship is touching in some form. There are endless qualities of touching. The wind is a relationship of warm air and cold air touching. All phenomenal effects are the results of the touching of divisional boundaries.

To show this relationship between the 2 points on the circumference, put them exactly together, one touching on top of the other. Crease the circle.

Any 2 points on the circumference of a circle, when touched together will fold the circle in half.

Marking 2 points on the circumference helps 5 and 6 year olds fold accurately. Young children are very good at putting small things together. This allows them to fold accurately from the start, something that otherwise would be difficult. It also works well for older students with a folding problem.

The folded line will always be at a <u>right-angle</u> to the direction of the folding movement, and will lie half way between the 2 points. Making 2 points generates more information because it started out with more information. *The right-angle movement of touching 2 points together and creasing the fold is fundamental to everything about folding circles.*

What new information is there now that was not there before the circle was folded?

Everything that is observed in folding the circumference is also there in folding using 2 points. A lot more information is revealed because we started with 2 points.

After folding the 2 points together we find 4 points, 2 end points of the diameter and the 2 points we started with. Use a pencil to draw lines connecting all 4 points on the circle. This shows the 12 specific relationships of each point to 3 others (4x3 = 12). Each of the 6 lines drawn between points represents 2 directions of relationship. There are 5 drawn lines; the folded line makes a sixth. The drawn line generate a fifth point of intersection on the diameter. The fifth point disappears when the circle is folded. The straight line relationship between the 2 marked points moves up into space away from the diameter as the 2 points are moved closer together. (see illustration below.) Three points remain on one plane and the fourth point moves off that plane forming 3 more triangular planes. The triangles drawn out on the circle do not change shape, the relationship of the 2 triangular planes changes as the circle is folded. Four points in space form a pattern of 4 triangular planes. Just folding a circle in half forms a transformational <u>tetrahedron</u> pattern.

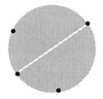 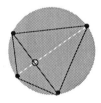 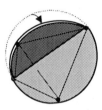  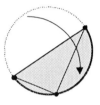

Flat circle with 4 points and diameter fold. | All points in relationship to each other. Five points when circle is flat. | Folding 2 points together forms a tetrahedron pattern, 5th point gone. | Continued folding changes proportion of tetrahedron pattern. | Circle in half, tetrahedron pattern gone, 3 points form a right-triangle.

The edge relationship of the first 2 points of the tetrahedron is <u>perpendicular</u>, at a right-angle to the diameter edge, the creased points, and represents the circular path of movement between the 2 points as they are folded together.

It is sometimes easier to see the tetrahedron form by folding the lines between the points making all the edges straight.

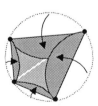   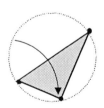

To check out the truth of this, place together and fold two points anywhere on the inside of the circumference. This will happen on any size or shape paper by folding two point together. It works with the circle, so it does with all that is less than a circle.

What information is there in the open flat circle?

There are now 6 lines with each end on the circumference. These correspond to the 6 edges of the tetrahedron. One is the diameter. Now, let's <u>count</u> the triangles.

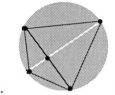 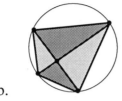 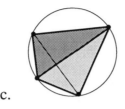 

a.　　　　　　　　b.　　　　　　　　c.　　　　　　　　d.

a. There are 8 individual triangles.
b. Here there are 2 sets of opposites, 4 <u>right-angle</u> triangles.
c. Here are 2 right-angle triangles.
d. Here are 2 <u>isosceles</u> triangles.
e. Two points exactly opposite each other half on the folded line is another diameter and froms a square. This is the only case where there will be 8 right-angle triangles.

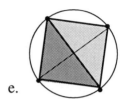

e.

What can we say about the right-angle triangles? Touching any 2 points together on the circumference will form a pattern of 6 right-angle triangles in the form of a <u>quadrilateral</u> shape, 4 on the diameter and 2 on the circumference, except when a square.

The end points of any diameter will form a right-angle triangle with any other point on the circumference. Compare all the circles by putting the folded right-triangles on top of each other. They are all congruent angles. The diameters will not line up. Every one put their points at different places on the circumference and each quadrilateral is differently proportioned. All being different they have the same number of right-triangles. The only exception is when the square is formed, otherwise there are only 2 right-angle triangles on the circumference, one on each side of the diameter.

Another point of interest is that everyone starts out with the same size circle and folds it in the same way. The process is the same for everyone. Each circle is folded the same way and every quadrilateral is proportionally different. No two are ever exactly the same. That shows how differences can arise from a consistent process where everyone is doing the same things.

I've had students put 2 points on the circumference a quarter of an inch apart, testing the theory. The results are a very long quadrilateral with a small width very close to one end of the diameter. The expression has dramatically changed. The process is unchanged and the information remains the same. The proportional relationship of parts is the difference; an effect of individual starting points.

Folding the circle into a 3-6 Pattern

There are only 3 different ways to proportionally fold the 1:2 folded circle again into a ratio of 1:2. Folding the circle generates triangulation. Wholeness plus 2 parts qualifies 3. We have seen how the first fold of the circle forms four points in triangulation. Three is principle to 4 in motion. Triangulation is principle formation of pattern, it happened first. It is reflected in all subsequent development. The triangle is the only structural relationship that exists. It is the only shape capable of holding itself rigid without collapsing. This section is about folding the circle into thirds. The 4 and 5 folding is the same process to different proportions.

Folding the hexagon pattern

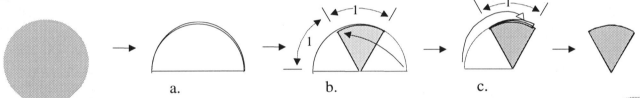

a. Fold the circle in a 1:2 ratio.
b. Fold that ratio again by folding the circumference once more to itself, moving one end point around until the folded part looks equal to the unfolded part. The folded edge line is half way between the opposite end point and the newly formed end point on the circumference. The 2 parts should look the same size. Do not measure; use your eyes to discern it proportionally.
c. Fold the unfolded end point behind to opposite folded point. Match up all the points, straight edges, and the circumference until everything is even. If edges are not even slide them back and forth until they are even. Only after everything is even, crease well with the straight edge. *It is important to make strong creases so the folds are sharp and easy to see. Crease the entire length of the circle. Weak creases make it difficult to see the points where lines intersect.*

The folded circle is a pie shape, a triangle pattern: it has 3 points and 3 sides, one side being the circumference. Any 3 points are a triangle pattern. The triangle shape is formed when the sides are connected with 3 straight lines. This folding is an <u>equilateral triangular pattern</u>. All 3 points are the same distance around. Check it out by comparing with other circles folded in the same way.

Let the folded circle fall open a bit and observe the curved edges in a zigzag folding, like a "Z". There is a duality of direction and interval. The folding is going in opposite directions. If the 2 end points are not opposite each other, one folded on top of the other, it is not folded correctly. This zigzag pattern is important, it reveals a triangulated pattern of 2 tetrahedra joined face to face. This in-and-out movement is fundamental to all the folding. It expresses the duality of the first fold in half.

a. Locate the 2 inside folded corners and slide them together. There is often surprise at what this produces, 2 tetrahedra joined edge to edge. The surprise lies in the unexpected transformation from such a simple movement. This is often a student's own discovery.

Unfold the circle making it flat.

a.

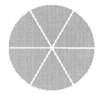

What information is there that was not there before the circle was folded?

It now has *3 diameters*. It is a circle shape divided into a <u>hexagon pattern</u>. Each diameter divides the other 2 in half, reflecting the ratio 1:2. This forms a <u>center point</u> to the circle. Each diameter is a <u>2-frequency</u> diameter. It is divided in 2 equal parts. Each part of the diameter is called a <u>radius,</u> a line that goes from center to the circumference.

The hexagon pattern is a <u>system</u> of 7 points, 6 on the circumference plus 1 in the center. The 6 sections, or <u>intervals</u>, formed by the diameters, together with the 7 points add up to a pattern of 13. Adding 3 diameters to 6 spaces and 7 points makes 16 parts, where 1+6 = 7, the hexagon division of the circle to itself. The number 13 is important and will soon be discussed at length (1+3 = 4). Remember the 4 sphere division into the tetrahedron pattern? Thirteen is the centered system of order and 4 is the primary non-centered system of order. It takes a minimum of 4 tetrahedra to form a pattern of 13 points in spherical order (3FA-25).

The 3 diameters plus the 7 points makes 10, the number of the tetrahedron, the first fold of the circle. Number patterns correlate to qualities of spatial pattern difficult to see otherwise.

It is important to have the students count specific parts, even older students. Counting is taken for granted as the students get older. They are taught to estimate. Students have trouble counting. They count the same parts and often come up with different answers. Counting forces them to look closer and that becomes a challenge.

Reforming the hexagon pattern

At this point in the folding it is important to explore what can be discovered using only the 3 folded diameters of the hexagon pattern. After about five minuets of investigation a classroom of students will have found all that is there. We then spend some time talking about what they came up with.

a. Tetrahedron

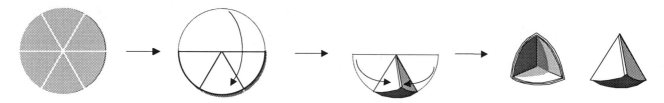

Fold the 2-frequency diameter circle in half. Fold the diameter on the 2 radial folds from center joining edges together. This reforms the circle into a triangular pyramid in a <u>tetrahedron</u> pattern. The 7 points of the hexagon pattern are rearranged, now 4 points in space, all equal distance from each other. The triangular space formed by the circumference joined together in thirds, forms the fourth triangle as the open base of the tetrahedral pattern.

b. Square base pyramid

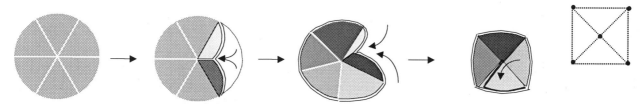

Open the circle flat and fold in on one radius, collapsing inward 2/6 (1/3) of the circle. Bring the 2 sections together forming a flap on the inside. Fold the flap flat against the inside. This forms a 4-sided concave space. The 5 points form a <u>quadrilateral</u> pyramid where the sides are triangular and the top point is the center of the circle.

c. Two tetrahedra joined by surface plane (bi-tetrahedral pattern)

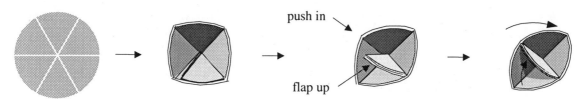

The quadrilateral pyramid will move on 2 axis perpendicular to each other. This reforms the <u>square</u> into an angle-shifting <u>parallelogram</u>. The square face moves into triangulation, becoming stable as the inside flap moves up to the opposite side forming a shared surface plane between the 2 tetrahedra.

d. Two tetrahedra joined by a common edge

From the 2 joined tetrahedra, open between the folded flap in the center, separating the center planes until you have 3 tetrahedra pattern joined by common edges. Continue to open until it shows a "crossing over" symmetry. We have seen another way to make this by sliding open the zigzag. A third way to form an open circle is to fold a diameter in half, joining the opposite end points together. This is a pattern of 6 points in space forming 2 tetrahedra and 2 tetrahedral intervals, a 4 tetrahedral pattern.

e. Tri-star

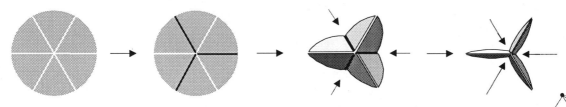

With the circle open flat, fold every other radius in and the other 3 folds will push out. This makes a star when viewed from the center point. It is 3 triangles joined on a central axis of 3 radius. The 5-point pattern of alternate folding in and out reveals 3 tetrahedra joined by common edge and planes.

f. Pentagon interval

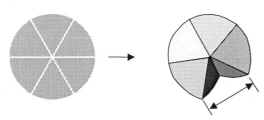

Fold in 1/3 of the circle half way until the interval is the same width as 1/6 of the circle. You then have a pentagon pattern.

g. Shapes

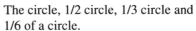

The circle, 1/2 circle, 1/3 circle and 1/6 of a circle.

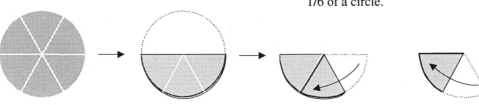

Explore all the configurations using only the 3 diameters. This information is fundamental to everything you will do in folding the circle. As the forms of the circle change, the proportions and symmetries become more complex, these functions of 3 diameters remain basic.

Spherical Vector Equilibrium

Each person in class folds 3 diameters, then folds one in half into 2 tetrahedra joined on a common edge, sometimes called a bow tie. We observe curved edges cross over on one side and diameters on the other side. We count the points, talk about methods of joining, and the importance of intervals

In pairs students figure out how to put 2 bow tie circles together in the same pattern as the single unit, <u>touching only on their straight edges</u>. This generates something new. In groups of 4 they put together 2 sets of 2 circles each, in the same way as before, touching only on the straight edges, without knowing beforehand that it will make a sphere. This is a great exploration for group problem solving.

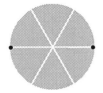
Fold ends of one diameter together

bobby pin
and hold closed with a bobby pin.

A single circle folded into a set of 2 tetrahedra joined on the edges, closed with a bobby pin. It is important to keep the symmetry.

Join **2 sets of 2 tetrahedra** reflecting the same pattern all around, generating a quadrilateral space collapsing on right angle axis.

plus

Join together **2 sets of 4 tetrahedra**, along the straight edges. Hold together with bobby pins as before. An open spherical pattern is formed.

This sphere is a Vector <u>Equilibrium</u> (**VE**) pattern. It shows both triangular and square intervals in an alternating pattern. The squares are a relationship of triangulation. Each edge defines both triangle and square.

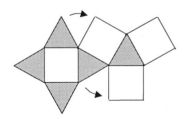

Describe and count parts:
- 4 circles
- 13 points
- 12 radii
- 36 equal edges
- 4 hexagon patterns
- 14 combined intervals
- 6 diameters, or axis
- 8 triangle spaces, tetrahedra
- 6 square spaces, inverted pyramid

Look at how the VE appears when sitting on a square opening and sitting on a triangular opening. Explain the difference.

We discuss our observations about the sphere and the process of making one. Start with the circle (O) Fold 1 diameter into 2 tetrahedra. Put 2 sets of 2 tetrahedra together getting 4 tetrahedra. Put 2 sets of 4 together getting a spherical pattern of 8. The sphere is complete. We write **O, 1, 2, 4, 8** on the board and talk about it as a progression of numbers, <u>Geometric Progression</u>. This spherical pattern is made from 8 tetrahedra; like an octave in music, everything fundamental is there. The parts are counted. One first grade student figured out how many square spaces, not by counting them, but by recalling the process. "We folded circles and put 2 of them together. That made 1 square. We put 2 of those things together and they made 4 squares. The 2 and the 4 made 6 squares." He was seeing a progressive process generating square intervals.

There are 13 points to the sphere, 12 around the center one. We talk about the number 13 and the connections we can make. Friday the 13th, bad luck, the clock with 12 around the center. We count 5 fingers, the forearm, all 6 point to the center of the palm making a pattern of 7. Six intervals complete a hexagon pattern of 13. We count the big movement joints of our bodies, 13 lunar months, a bakers dozen, etc.

Spherical matrix

All edges of the VE are the same length. If the points were centers of spheres there would be 12 spheres and one in the middle, a system of 13 spheres. Any one of these spheres can be the center for another interrelated system of 13. This can be extended indefinitely. This is the order of the closest packing of spheres of the same size. It is a <u>matrix</u> in which all fundamentally patterned systems can be found. The VE is the centered system of spherical order. The tetrahedron is non-centered. The first fold of the circle is tetrahedral. It takes 4 tetrahedra to form the same VE pattern that is formed from 4 circles. It is all about formation of endless design within spherical order.

There are 3 definitive positions from which to view the symmetry of the VE matrix; from the triangle face/ hexagon, the square face, and from any point. The point symmetry shows a duality of 2 squares and 2 triangles. We shall see later how 2 squares are the 2 halves of one octahedron and the 2 triangles are 2 tetrahedra. Two tetrahedra make one octahedron. The point viewing of the VE shows a proportional balance of 2 tetrahedra.

1. **The Tetrahedron**

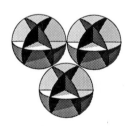 plus equals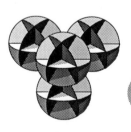

Put 3 VEs touching point to point all in single orientation, or facing in the same direction. Add the fourth sphere, consistent to direction, between the first 3 completing a tetrahedral pattern. The tetrahedron is the radial lines from center point to center point. The curved openings show the octahedron pattern. Notice that the pattern of points and planes is different on the bottom of the three than it is on the top. Use bobby pins and or tape to hold them together.

2. The Octahedron

Start with 3 formed VE spheres in a triangle, all in the same orientation. Put a triangle of 3 more on top. The 2 sets of 3 VEs are in opposite direction while individually the spheres remain consistent in the same direction. These 6 VE spheres form an <u>octahedron</u> pattern from center to center. (3FA-11).

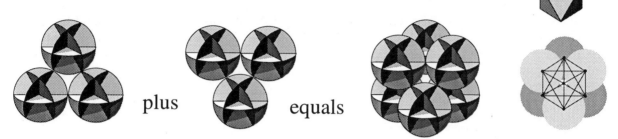

3. The Vector Equilibrium (VE)

Thirteen spheres will form a VE pattern (3FA-25). There are 3 layers; 3 on the bottom, 7 in the middle and 3 on the top. For the strongest joining interlock the bobby pins and use tape across joints.

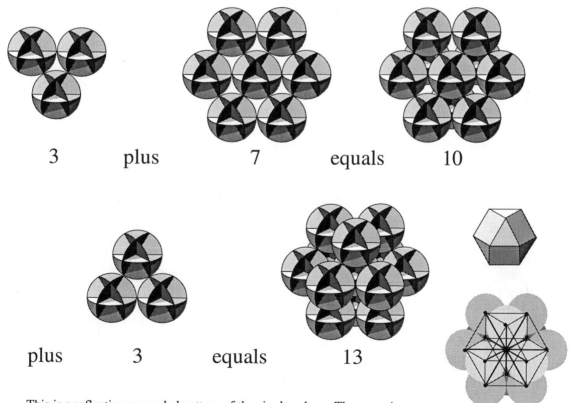

This is a reflective expanded pattern of the single sphere. There are 4 great circles, each a hexagon pattern where they all share the center location. It is traditionally called the cuboctahedron (p. 34).

4. The Cube

The cube pattern is a non-center spherical system of order. It shows 14 spheres in a different arrangement than the VE, which is only one sphere less. The VE is a 3-7-3 layered arrangement while the cube is a 5-4-5 layered arrangement. In both cases they are separated aspects from the same matrix of the closest packing, most stable order of spheres (p. 50) The spheres are the same size, each is an exact reflection of the other. This forms an endless multiplicity that is the order of divisional patterns and the forming of endless designs. It is an order that is whole, reflected in spherical form. It is the same wholeness of order and pattern development that is compressed into the dynamics of the circle. Through folded circles the pattern of spherical order can be unfolded.

Within this spherical matrix, space is defined between the spheres. When the centers of the spaces are connected a cubic matrix will emerge. There is an amazing amount of ordered relationships revealed when considering the center of spheres, the points of touching and the center of the spaces defined by the spheres.

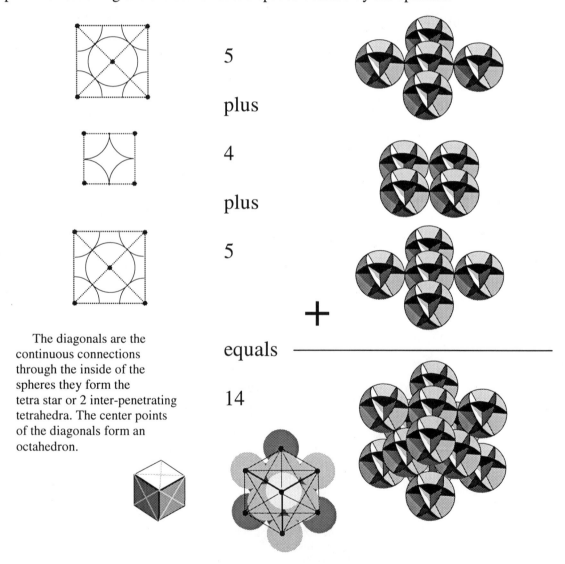

The diagonals are the continuous connections through the inside of the spheres they form the tetra star or 2 inter-penetrating tetrahedra. The center points of the diagonals form an octahedron.

64

Equilateral triangle

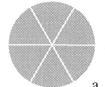 a. 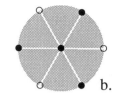 b. 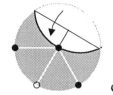 c.  d.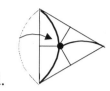

a. Start by folding the 3 diameters.
b. Mark the center point and every second point on the circumference.
c. Fold one circumference point right onto the center point. The diameter will line up with itself. Crease the fold well with a straight edge.
d. Fold the other 2 alternating radial points to the center. Each diameter has been folded once to the center point forming an <u>equilateral triangle</u>. If the triangle isn't accurate, it might be the diameters weren't folded accurately.

1. **The Right Triangle**

   Turn the equilateral triangle over so curved edges are on the bottom. Each diameter makes a right-angle division of each edge length in half, making a <u>2-frequency</u> equilateral triangle. Count the number of <u>right-angle triangles</u>. Usually the 6 small ones get counted, the large ones go unnoticed. There are 12 all together, 6 large and 6 ones.

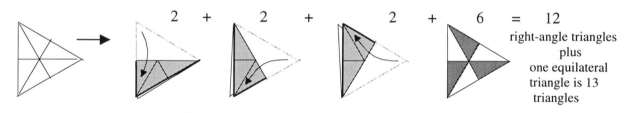

2 + 2 + 2 + 6 = 12 right-angle triangles plus one equilateral triangle is 13 triangles

   To experience the right-angle triangles, fold the equilateral triangle in half on each bisector line, one at time. Do this in all 3 directions revealing 6 congruent large right-angle triangles, in 3 sets of opposites, 3 right-handed right angle triangles and 3 left-handed right-angle triangles. Within each of the 6 large right triangles there are 3 smaller right-angle triangles of the same size.

   Have students work together exploring different arrangements of right and left-hand right-angle triangles. Two congruent triangles of the same handedness will always form a parallelogram. A right-hand and left-hand triangle will not.

2. **The Hexagon**

    After folding the 3 diameters open the circle flat. The 6 lines forming the hexagon shape on the circumference were creased by folding the 3 bisectors of the triangle. The 2-frequency equilateral triangle is simply another form of a hexagon pattern. There are 3 sides and each is divided in half making 6 equal sections on the perimeter. It is the right-angle symmetry of the equilateral triangles and the diameter bisectors that make it work.

3. Two ways to fold the circle in half

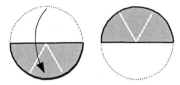

a. The obvious way is to fold a circle in 2 congruent parts; 180° on each side of the fold.

b. Given that the sum of the inside angles of a triangle is 180°, half a circle, folding an entire circle into an equilateral triangle is also 2 sides, each is 180°.

 ## Down folding the hexagon

Fold in on the 6 chords forming the hexagon shape.

Fold the hexagon in half on one of the diameters. It forms a quadrilateral shape called a <u>trapezoid</u>, having only one set of parallel edges.

Fold over one of the triangles using the crease, forming another kind of quadrilateral called a <u>parallelogram</u>.

Fold one equilateral triangle onto the other.

This shows the placement of the folded parallelogram in the circle. This parallelogram (2 pairs of parallel sides, all equal) has a specific name, called a <u>Rhomboid</u>. It shows 2 equilateral and 2 isosceles triangles sharing the perpendicular dividers.

Fold one right triangle onto the other.

Here we see the entire circle folded into the single shape of a right-handed right angle triangle. Showing images of polygons and other separated shapes, we forget they are part of a context. They are the results of the whole circle movement towards individualization. One advantage of folding circles is that the wholeness of the circle remains. It is the unity of the Whole that allows for the transformational connections between diverse shapes and forms. Systems are the configurations of the circle grid in self-multiplicity.

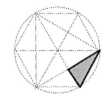

Right angle tetrahedron puzzle

a. The equilateral triangle folded in half forms 2 right triangles.
b. Form an <u>isosceles triangle</u> by folding over the right-angled corner on the folded line, then unfold.
c. Fold the <u>acute</u> corner on the other folded line forming a quadrilateral.
d. Fold in first right angle to edge of second folding over on middle fold of isosceles triangle. Tape the 2 edges together.
e. Fold 3 circles as shown and arrange them together in a way to form a complete tetrahedron. This is a good problem solver.

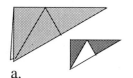 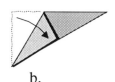 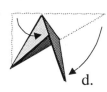
a. b. c. d. e.

 The tetrahedron

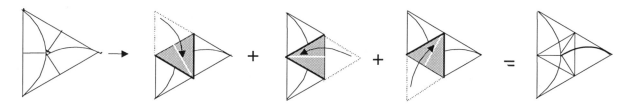

a. Starting with the folded equilateral triangle (3FA-5), fold each corner point to midpoint on the opposite edge. Complete each fold individually, fold one then unfold it and fold the next one, unfold that and fold the third one, with points right onto points. Do not fold triangles on top of each other as they will bunch causing inaccuracies.

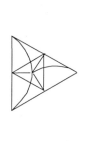 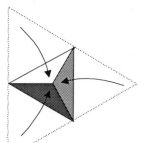

b. Next, fold the 3 corner points together at the top, forming a new corner point. Tape along the edges to hold tetrahedron together. Count 4 end points, 4 triangular surfaces, and 6 edges of the tetrahedron.

Look at point, line, and plane symmetries of the tetrahedron. Observe the right-angle axial rotation that occurs around any 2 opposite edges.

Notice how the 4 points define 2 sets of 3 edges, each define the full tetrahedron pattern. Each set reveals an opposite spiral movement, one is right-handed and the other is left-handed. This is again an expression of duality as a principle quality inherent to the first movement of the circle.

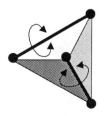

2-Frequency tetrahedron

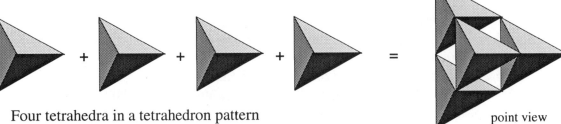

point view

Four tetrahedra in a tetrahedron pattern reveal an octahedron space not seen in a single tetrahedron. All tetrahedra are in the same orientation, joined point to point. 4 triangles and 4 triangular intervals define this open space. An octahedron made from 2 open tetrahedra will fit perfectly into this space making it "solid".

The 2-frequency tetrahedron has 10 points, 6 of connection and 4 end points. This reflects four spheres in order. A solid tetrahedron is missing 6 tangent points of information.

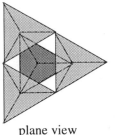

plane view

edge view

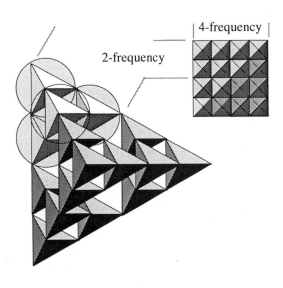

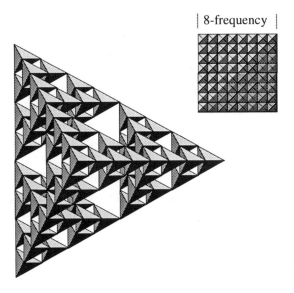

Four tetrahedra in a tetrahedron pattern form a 2-frequency tetrahedron, four 2-frequency tetrahedra in a tetrahedron pattern form an 8-frequency tetrahedron, and four 8's form a 16-frequency tetrahedron, and so on.

    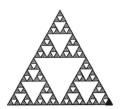

All 4 faces of the tetrahedron show the same development of frequency. The division of pattern generates an endless multiplication of spatial intervals. Pattern is without scale. This image is sometimes called Sirpinski's Triangle.

Pascal's Triangle

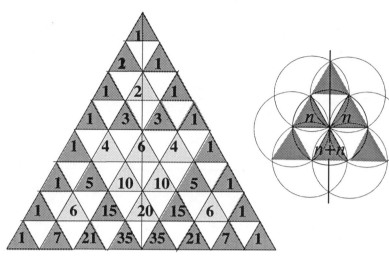

Pascal's Triangle is a number function based on the hexagon pattern in a triangular bilateral form of circular order. It is an interesting horizontal and diagonal sequences of number relationships. The numbers work only in the triangles with the same orientation. The descending values in horizontal rows are determined by a hexagon cell from one row to the next. Starting with the top hexagon, 1+ 1 = 2. Note that all the odd numbers are dark. The even numbers are in the center white of the Sirpinski Triangle.

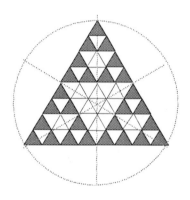

When looking at the design of things it is necessary to look for the unseen connections that allow us to see the non-formed pattern. In the image to the left it is simply done by connecting edge lines to complete the triangular grid, and points to see the diameters. In a folded circle the pattern grid is always visible. With increased frequency comes increased possibilities of diverse design combinations. The hexagon is the most fundamental <u>tessellating</u> grid; an arrangement of shapes that fill a surface without gaps or overlap.

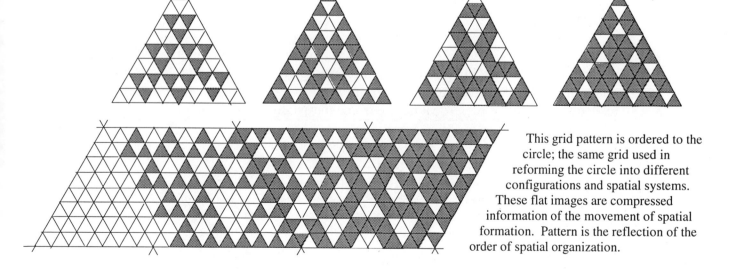

This grid pattern is ordered to the circle; the same grid used in reforming the circle into different configurations and spatial systems. These flat images are compressed information of the movement of spatial formation. Pattern is the reflection of the order of spatial organization.

3FA-11 Octahedron

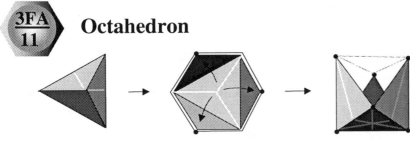

tetrahedron half open

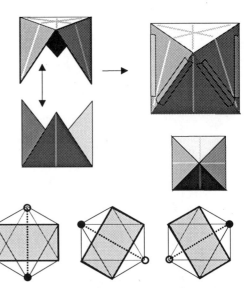

Open the tetrahedron half way showing 4 triangle spaces the same size as the 4 triangles that form them. This makes an octahedron pattern of 6 end points and 8 triangle intervals. Using 2, the triangles of one fit exactly into the spaces of the other completing the octahedron form. Tape edges together.

Relationship of 3 individual squares, seen as rectangles, and 3 axes perpendicular to the square planes.

Counting parts of the octahedron, we find 6 points, 3 axis, 8 equilateral triangles, and looking at it from each end, point 3 squares. Again the square is revealed as a relationship generated from triangles.

When you tape the edges of the 2 tetrahedra together it reveals a zigzag of 6 edges continuously around a center band of 6 triangles of the octahedron. The top triangle is in opposite orientation to the bottom triangle. It is a primary anti-prism pattern (3FA-75). This happens in 4 different directions reflecting a tetrahedral symmetry.

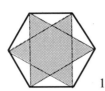 1.    2.

One view of the 6 edges of the octahedron showing (1) from the top and (2) from the side.

Draw from different points of view what you make 3-dimensionally. Model what you draw. Write about both what you model and what you draw. Give number expression to what you understand. This gives you 4 different ways of viewing the same information. Each is a good check on the other.

Divide the class in half. One half has tetrahedra, the other octahedra. Each half has the same problem to solve. Put 4 tetrahedra into a tetrahedron pattern; put 4 octahedra into a tetrahedron pattern. They will regroup into fours, coming back together to share what they have discovered; the reciprocal nature of the tetrahedron and octahedron.

All-space organizing tetrahedron/octahedron matrix

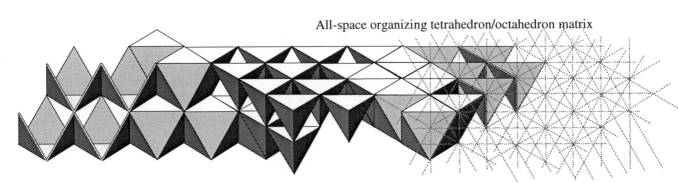

Octahedra in tetrahedron pattern

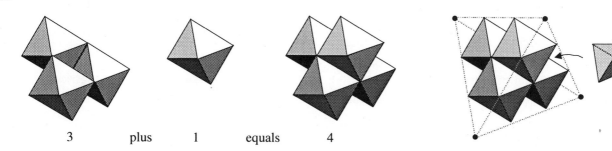

3   plus   1   equals   4

Have students put 4 octahedra into a tetrahedron pattern (3 on the bottom, one on top in same orientation, joined edge to edge). By extending an invisible line connecting the end points of the octahedra, you can see the 6 edges of a 3-frequency tetrahedron. Notice the intervals are all tetrahedral, even the inverted one in the center. *Tetrahedra form octahedron intervals, octahedra form tetrahedron intervals.* Duality reveals itself in a reciprocal patterned function of form and interval.

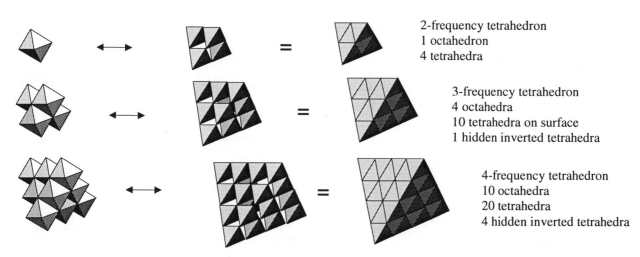

2-frequency tetrahedron
1 octahedron
4 tetrahedra

3-frequency tetrahedron
4 octahedra
10 tetrahedra on surface
1 hidden inverted tetrahedra

4-frequency tetrahedron
10 octahedra
20 tetrahedra
4 hidden inverted tetrahedra

What are the next quantities in this number sequence of octahedra and tetrahedra development?

2-frequency octahedron

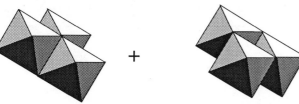 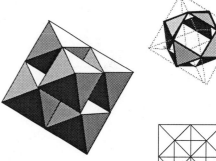

Join 6 octahedra, in 2 sets of 3 on their edges. This forms a 2-frequency octahedron with 8 tetrahedron intervals in a VE pattern (3FA-18).

71

Students will need time to explore different combinations of tetrahedra and octahedra and how they are parts of the VE sphere. This is good folding practice and allows them to use what they are learning to find out what works and what doesn't. It is important for them to explore the congruent parts, the intervals, and the development of shapes and forms in the circle. Some get into elaborate coloring on the surface of the forms. As a group we look at what everyone has worked on and how what they did will fit together, making larger and more complex parts. Some of them keep with the matrix pattern some do not. Below are a few examples of things that have been made.

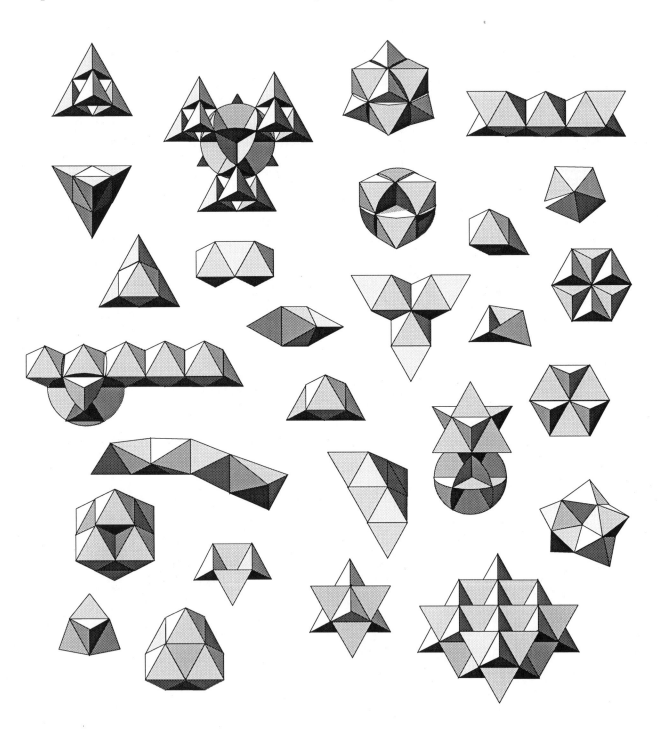

Triangle, 4, 5 and 6

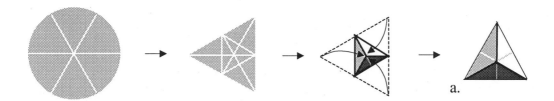

a. Fold the circle into a tetrahedron (3FA-8).

b. By opening it from the end point proportional intervals of the square (4), a pentagon (5) and hexagon (6) can be generated. This allows objects to be formed with 4, 5, and 6 fold symmetries.

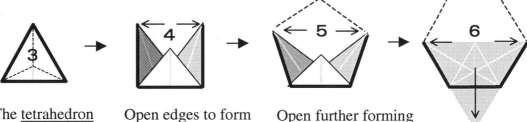

The <u>tetrahedron</u> edges show 4 closed triangles.

Open edges to form a *square* interval. Join 2 opened tetrahedra edge to edge forming an <u>octahedron</u> of 8 triangles.

Open further forming a *pentagon* interval. Joining 7 circles with some triangles over lapping will form an <u>icosahedron</u> of 20 triangles.

Opening the triangle flat forms half a *hexagon*. Two triangles make a hexagon.

   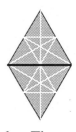

c. These are the only 3 regular polyhedra made from equilateral triangles. The octahedron and icosahedron can be formed from the angles by opening the tetrahedron and being joined to the same angulation of itself. Another way of forming an icosahedron is by using only 2 folded circles (3FA-44).

    The cube is the fourth regular polyhedron and is formed using 6 squares made from 4 right-angle tetrahedra (3FA-90) or 2 circles folded into the 4-8 pattern (4FA-6).

    The Dodecahedron is the fifth of the regular polyhedra. It is formed from 12 pentagons made by joining pentacaps (3FA-45) or 2 circles folded into the 5-10 pattern (3FA-7).

    These 5 regular polyhedra are fundamental pattern components for spatial organization found throughout nature. Common to all is triangulation, the triangle.

Tetrahedron star

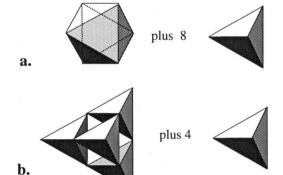
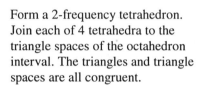
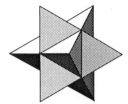
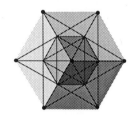

a. Put one tetrahedron on each of the 8 octahedron faces, joining surfaces. This will form a <u>stellated octahedron</u> or sometimes called a tetrastar.

b. Form a 2-frequency tetrahedron. Join each of 4 tetrahedra to the triangle spaces of the octahedron interval. The triangles and triangle spaces are all congruent.

The <u>tetrastar</u> is 2 intersecting 2-frequency tetrahedra sharing the same octahedron center. This is a <u>cubic pattern</u>. Each of the 8 corner points of the tetrastar are the corners of the cube, and the right-angle crossing of the edges of the tetrahedra are the diagonals on the 6 square faces of the cube.

Viewing the cube pattern from 3 places of symmetry:

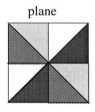 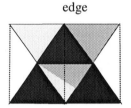 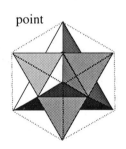 

plane   edge   point

3-frequency tetrastar

Tetrahedron inside out

a. Open a tetrahedron out flat to the circle.
b. Refold the tetrahedron leaving the curved edges out instead of folding the equilateral triangle.
c. Fold the 3 corner points of the large triangle together forming the tetrahedron with curved flaps out.

curves folded on inside

curves folded on outside

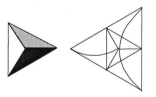   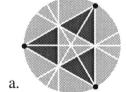   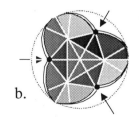 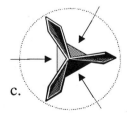

a.   b.   c.

Tetrahedron inside out, 2-frequency

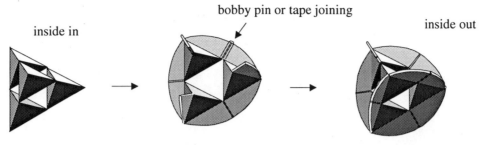

a. 2-frequency tetrahedron

b. Three inside-out tetrahedra are put into a triangular arrangement, joining on the straight edges of the outside flaps. Either use tape or bobby pins to hold them.

c. The fourth inside-out tetrahedron is placed on top, again joining on the straight edges of the flaps.

Tetrastar inside out

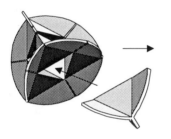
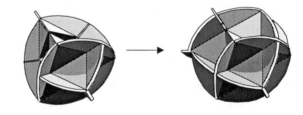

d. Start with the 2-frequency tetrahedron inside out.

e. Place bottom of one inside-out tetrahedron congruent to one of the triangular spaces. The straight edges of the flaps will join perpendicular to the joint of the other flaps.

f. Do the same thing with 3 more inside-out tetrahedra, joining them all in the same way, covering each triangular space. The circumference on the outside reveals more information.

This spherical pattern has 12 <u>rhombic</u> planer spaces, it is a <u>Rhombidodecahedron</u> pattern (5FA-11). It has 14 outside points which reveal the cube pattern of 14 spheres in the closest packed order (3FA-4, 4). The 14 outside points of edge intersections reveal both the 6 points of the octahedron and the 8 points of the cube.

Three different views of symmetry that are found in the spherical rhombidodecahedron.

75

Tetrahelix

a. Start with one tetrahedron.
b. Place another on it.
c. Place a third next to it on any face. Look for the symmetry of this set of 3.
d. Make another set of 3 the same way and join them so that there is a long edge forming where the edge of one set lines up with the edge of the other set, together making three 2-frequency edges. These 3 edges will be twisting in the same direction.

a.

b.

c.

d.

e.

f.

A helix is formed by putting tetrahedra in a line face to face.

Depending how the 2 sets were placed together, the twist will be to the right or to the left.

e. Make another set of 3 tetrahedra, add in the same way as before in (d.) This will extend the twisting edges to 9 tetrahedra.
f. Add another set of 3, staying consistent with the direction of the twist, making it 12 tetrahedra.

Transformational Tetrahelix

There is a much more interesting way to form a tetrahelix. Start with one tetrahedron and bring an edge together with the edge of another tetrahedron, using a taped hinge (p. 28). This makes a set of two tetrahedra. Join two sets of two together in the same way making a set of four tetrahedra joined on opposite edges. Join this set of four to another set of four using the same hinge joint, making a complete hinged set of eight.

Each tetrahedron is joined to the other on opposite edges; all are perpendicular to each other in a line. This tetrahelix moves in many different ways.

 1 tetrahedron

 1 set of 2 tetrahedra

 2 sets of 2, 4 tetrahedra

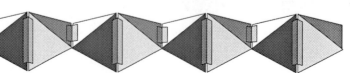 2 sets of 4, 8 tetrahedra

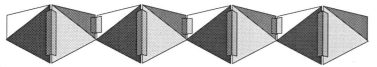

a. Twist the line of tetrahedra to the right until all the tetrahedra are face to face forming a right-hand helix. "Untwist" tetrahelix, open the line then twist to the left. It will continue to spin right.

b. Mark all the tetrahedra faces in the same way on the outside of the helix, so you can follow the movement of the faces as they are rearranged. The marked faces can all be hidden on the inside, all exposed on the outside, and half in and half out. With half in and half out the spin of the helix will be reversed from the other 2. This can not be seen unless marked in some way.

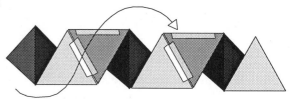

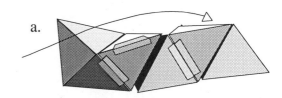

a.

Right hand directional spin, all outside faces to outside and change to same faces on the inside.

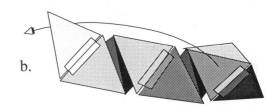

b.

Spin in opposite direction with half faces inside and half outside.

3FA 21 Torus Ring

a. Bring one end of the tetrahelix around to the opposite end and hinge join the edges together forming a circle.

This line of 8 tetrahedra in a circle is an octave, like 8 tetrahedra of the VE sphere. 8 is the least amount of tetrahedra that will form a circle end to end forming a <u>torus</u> that will roll through its own center.

It is easier to see the movement when faces are different colors.

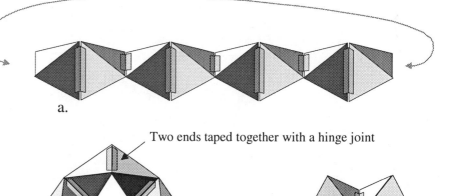

Two ends taped together with a hinge joint

Three positions of transformation

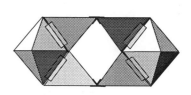

2-Frequency Tetrahelix

This is easier than it looks. The flat image of the helix is harder to understand than the actual model where spatial organization is not compressed and distorted.

a.

a. Make a 2-frequency tetrahedron (3FA-9) using 4 individual tetrahedra.

b. Follow the procedure for making a tetrahelix (3FA-19). Start with joining two 2-frequency tetrahedra face to face. Tape edges.

b.

c. Join 2 sets of 2, face to face. Depending on how they are joined, The tetrahedra will twist to the right or the left.

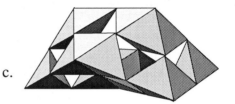
c.

d. Join 2 sets of 4 in the same direction, taping along edges.

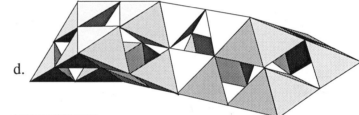
d.

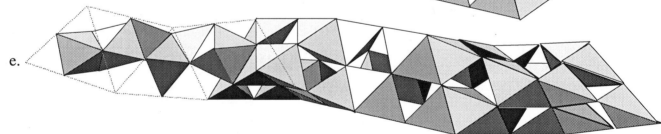
e.

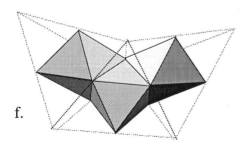
f.

e. When the space inside the tetrahelix is realized as a pattern of connected octahedra, it can then be formed revealing another level of helix formation.

f. The relationship of octahedra is clearly seen in the symmetry of three tetrahedra joined face to face. It has no directional movement until a forth is added.

3FA-23 Double helix

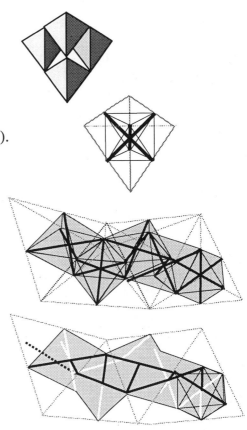

a. Tie a piece of string to the mid-points between opposite edges of the tetrahedron. Do this 3 times showing the 3 axial connections between the opposite end points of the octahedron (3FA-11).

b. Do this to all individual 2-frequency tetrahedra in the helix form. In looking at 3 tetrahedra/octahedra we see how the axis of the octahedra connect one to the other.

c. There are 2 continuous strands that connect through the length of the helix. Paint those strands and the perpendicular string connecting the strands the same color. You will have painted half the axial lines of each octahedron interval in a continuous pattern. This half axis is the pattern for the DNA double helix ladder.

3FA-24 Octahelix

Any antiprism (FA-75) stacked to itself, base to base, will form a helix movement by following the edges as they spiral around the form. The tetrahelix is different in that it has no opposing bases to join together.

a. Make the octahedron shown in (3FA-76c).

b. Put 3 octahedra into this pattern. This is a little more difficult, as the orientation of the open octahedron changes as it spirals around.

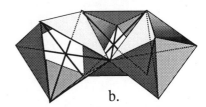

c. Make three sets of three in the same way and put them together to repeat the pattern as they lie inside the tetrahelix. This is an easy form in which to tape string or glue sticks to see the axis inside the octahedron.

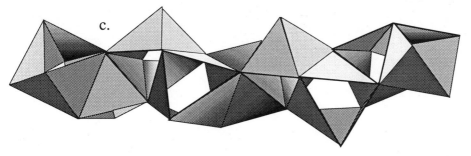

Vector Equilibrium/Cuboctahedron

Join 8 tetrahedra so they all share a common center point. You will find they have to be placed edge to edge, 4 in one direction that generate intervals for 4 in the opposite direction. The symmetry is 3, 4, and 6. The hexagon pattern of the circle is to itself 4 times in equilibrium. The symmetrical balance is the 3 and 4, just as the 10 points of the tetrahedron is 4 triangles and 3 squares. The straight-line edges are the result of circular relationships of spherical order.

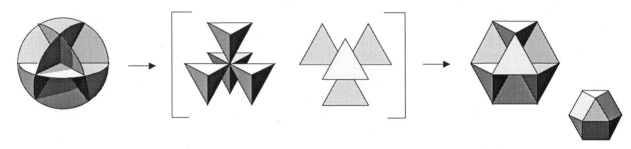

Four tetrahedra is the minimum centered system (13 points in space). They are also the minimum non-centered systems (10 points, the 2- frequency tetrahedron). The full spherical Vector Equilibrium pattern is always 13 spheres, 4 circles, and 4 tetrahedra in order. This pattern is at the same time the sphere, the cube, and octahedron forming a tetrahedral patterned grid. The solid VE form is the truncation of both the cube and octahedron (see p. 34, 35). More importantly this pattern is the matrix order of spatial organization.

a. Putting eight right angle tetrahedra (3FA-90) into the tetrahedral spaces with the right-angle corners pointing out forms a 2-frequency cube.

b. Putting 6 octahedra into the 6 square intervals in the VE forms a 2-frequency octahedron.

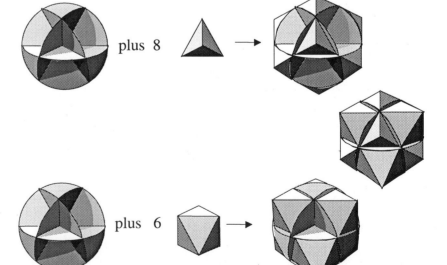

6 octahedra form 8 tetrahedral intervals

Four hexagons are shown below, each in a different orientation. This is the same hexagon pattern of 4 folded circles joined in combination with each other to form the VE spherical pattern. The 4 circles are called "great circles" because they lie on the surface of a sphere and the plane goes through the center of the sphere (3FA-3). To cut through a sphere not through the center will reveal a circle less than the circumference; they would be called "lessor circles."

There are only 6 axial diameters in the VE, half the number of points on the great circles. The center point is defined in common by all the center points of the 4 circles.

Nesting of one form inside another is a traditional way of seeing the relationship of individual polyhedra within each other. Within the 4-frequency tetrahedron is the 2-frequency octahedron in which there is a one frequency VE. The VE is 4 tetrahedra in single orientation. Each tetrahedra is 4 spheres that is the 13 spheres that reveal the tetrahedron and octahedron matrix of order. The nesting pattern demonstrates organized interrelated fractal design where levels of frequency and orientation are the primary means of connections. Nesting of these polyhedra is only a reflection of the closest packed order of spheres that are the same size.

Four squared tetrahedra

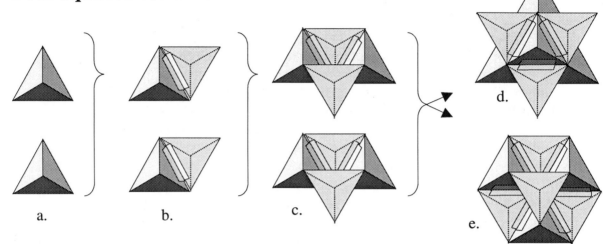

a. Make two tetrahedra (3FA-8).
b. Join them edges to edges. Tape on both sides making a hinge joint.
c. Join 2 sets of 2 together, edges to edges forming a square interval.
   Notice the different between the top and bottom. One is an inverted square pyramid and the other shows a perpendicular crossing of 2 edge lines.
d. Join 2 sets of 4 tetrahedra; square edges to square edges. This forms 8 tetrahedra in a tetrastar form, a cube pattern. The inside space forms an octahedron interval (3FA-12).
e. Join 2 sets of 4 tetrahedra by joining the crossing of edges opposite the square.
   This forms a vector equilibrium or cuboctahedron pattern.

 Tetrahedron fractal

Fractals are a function of organized form changing within the unchanging nature of pattern generation. It happens as a flat function because it happens in space. It is clearly seen as a primary function of division into the tetrahedron/octahedron matrix. Movement is always in 2 directions, it is expansion as well.

a. We will start by looking at the tetrastar.
   The primary triangle is divided into 2-frequency.

b. The next step will be to divide all the triangle faces into 2-frequency triangles making it a 4-frequency star. This is done by making tetrahedra one half the size of the larger ones. Do this by determining the diameter of a smaller circle that will fold into the correct size tetrahedron.

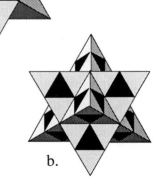

c. Start with half the tetrastar, 4 tetrahedra in a square pattern.

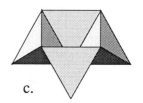

d. Make 4 smaller tetrahedron the size of half of each of the 12 triangular faces and put them into the square interval edge to edge, with faces to the faces of the larger triangles.

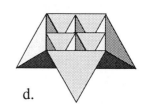

e. Make 4 more smaller tetrahedra as before and put the to the faces of the outside triangles completing the 4-frequency edge crossings.

f. Make 8 more small tetrahedra and put them to the remaining triangle faces. This makes 14 smaller tetrahedra that have been added. Turn it over and notice that now the top and bottom are the same form. They are the same pattern as the tetrastar. There are now 4 tetrastars and the relative size has changed.

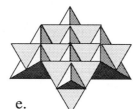

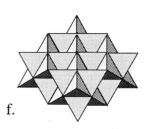

g. Make another unit exactly the same and put them together into a tetrastar pattern (3FA-9d). Notice how it is beginning to fill out the cubic pattern and at the same time creating a lot more square intervals, which are smaller octahedra spaces. This is a pattern that happens throughout, not just on the outside.

h. Go through the same process again making the individual tetrahedra 1/2 times smaller making the next level of development 8-frequency.

i. This shows three squares that have a frequency increase where the entire pattern would be 16-frequency for the triangles that form the tetrastar.

Octahedron fractal

a.

Proportional scaling of the tetrahedron demonstrates an aspect of pattern formation that is called fractals. It happens with the octahedron as shown here, and in all formations that adhere to a non-changing pattern while remaining consistent in form generating on different scales. Irregular forms become restrictive in development in the same scale and through proportional scaling large and small will continue to generate.

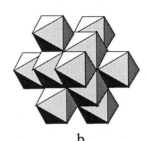
b.

a. Start with an octahedron.

b. Make 8 smaller octahedra to a one-half proportion of the first octahedra. Put them face to face on the first octahedron dividing it into a 2-frequency octahedron.

c. Continue the process and figure out how many smaller octahedra of what size will be needed to develop the next higher frequency. Each triangular surface is again divided in half by a smaller scale of the same forming.

d. Here only the tetrahedron pattern is emerging as it is developed by higher frequency formation.

e. Here we see successive scaling of the 4 sizes of octahedra as the are placed one onto the other, or in the case of nature one that develops out from the other.

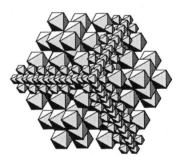
d.

e.

Area of rectangle/triangle

The area of a rectangle can be understood within the context of triangulation. The tetrahedron is primary triangle formation.

a. Make a tetrahedron. Tape only 2 edges leaving one edge open.
b. Push on the 2 ends of the untaped edges and they will open.
c. As the triangle sides are pushed they will begin to bend.
d. Crease the sides as the endpoints of the edge get closer.
e. Flatten into a rectangle. The base and height of both the triangle and the rectangle are the same.
f. Fold the rectangle in half and look at the creased triangles.
g. Fold one of the triangles back over and notice how creases line up.
h. From the large rectangle fold a corner right-triangle over.
i. Fold both corner triangles over to join edges in the middle. This makes half the form of the original tetrahedron.
j. Fold back to the rectangle, pushing open corners back together reforming the initial tetrahedron.

a.

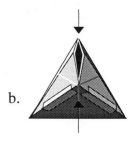
b.

c.

d.

 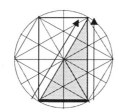

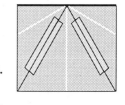
e.

The area of the rectangle and the triangle can be understood in the context of the 4-frequency diameter circle. The base width of a rectangle is the length of both bottom and top. The height is the distance the base moves from bottom to top. **Base X Height = Area of Rectangle**.

The base of a triangle diminishes in length as it moves up to a point. From the base to point is the height or <u>altitude</u>. There is only one base length at the bottom of the triangle and 2 for the rectangle. **1/2 Base X Height = Area of triangle.** When the tetrahedron is flattened to a rectangle with folded triangles, the relationship becomes clear. With what can be understood form the transformable tetrahedron, it is then relatively easy to figure out the volume of the tetrahedron.

j. 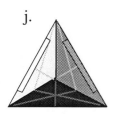   i. 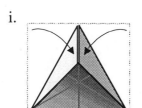   h. 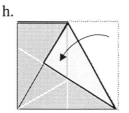   g. 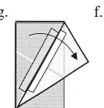   f.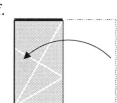

Tetratube transformation

a. Start with the tetrahedron that has been taped on only 2 edges (3FA-29).
b. Flatten the tetrahedron (3FA-29b-e)
c. Cut along the creased edge that is parallel to the open edge.
d. Open it into a square. Notice how unstable it is in this open form compared to the enclosed form of the tetrahedron.

This transformation of the tetrahedron into a square tube is a good demonstration of the right-angle movement and the division of right-angle triangles. It is one of the few times that the circle is cut into. It is only done for demonstration purposes. When the 2 edges are untaped the circle will fall into 2 separate pieces. The whole having been cut becomes limited.

e. There are 4 sets of right-angle triangles: 4 right and 4 left hand triangles. The 4 corners of the tetrahedron are now 8 corner points.
f. Push the corner where the tape comes together to the opposite corner closing the square to a pointed straight edge.
g. Bring the opposite end square corners together in the same way. This makes 2 quadrilateral planes; folding kite shapes that intersect each other through the center lines. The 4 right-angle corners form a tetrahedron pattern.
h. Fold the cut end of the tube back to a straight edge again.
i. Fold the opposite end in the same way at right-angle to the other end forming the regular tetrahedron, from where all this started.

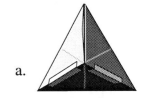

a.

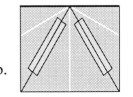

b.

The diagonal of the rectangle side is equal to the tetrahedron edge length. The surface area remains the same. The volume of the tetrahedron changes when changed into the rectangular tube.

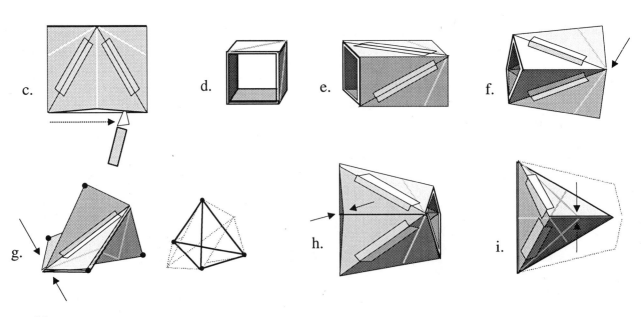

Tetratube development

a. Reform the tetrahedron (3FA-30g).
b. Make another one the same way.
c. Join them together, open end to open end. Move at right-angles to each other until the become congruent forming an octahedron. The flaps form a tetrahedron. Count a pattern of 10 points.

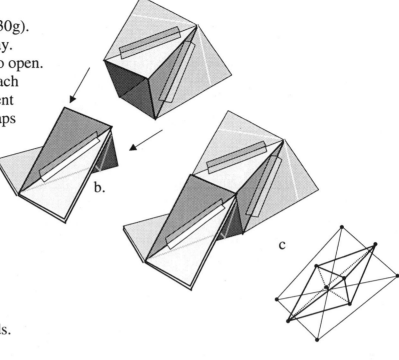

d. Fold the 2 flaps on one end together and tape on short ends.
e. Do the same to the other side.

f. The opposite handedness is formed by taping flaps in opposite direction.

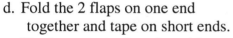

There are many ways to put these units together, as there are many different variations of configurations for each unit.

g. This is one of a number of helix formations that can be made.
h. A circle design using multiples of a single unit.
Linear, planer and circle/spherical systems can be formed using combinations of folds.

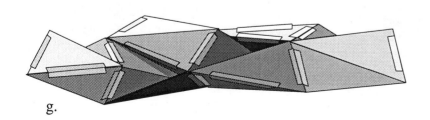

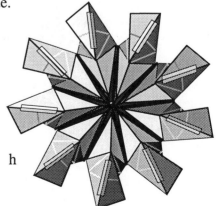

Octahedron movement system

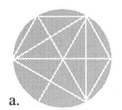
a.
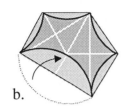
b.

c.

d.

e.

a. Fold hexagon pattern, one large triangle and 4 of the 6 hexagon sides.
b. Fold 1/3 unfolded hexagon on the triangle base line forming a pentagon shape.
c. Fold on centerline. Bring one side of hexagon to inside line of the large triangle.
d. Fold isosceles triangle overlapping previously folded side bringing edges together.
e. Tape along overlapping edges.

Twelve of these tetrahedra will be needed for this system. With 6 the overlap fold (c) and (d) will be to the right, 6 with overlap to the left. They will all be joined using hinge joints (p. 28). The pattern for joining is the same throughout.

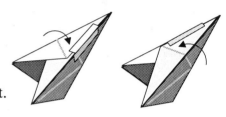

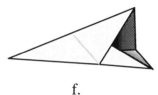
f.
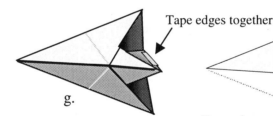
g.
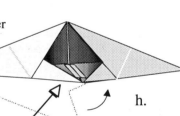
h.

Tape edges together

Tape edges on other side

f. Start with one tetrahedral unit.
g. Join 2 faces together, with opposite overlapping symmetry. Tape along edges
h. Open all the way so adjacent edges meet. Tape opposite side of taped joint. It is now a set of 2 hinged joined on a single axial edge.

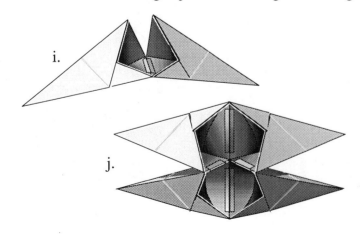
i.
j.

i. Make another set of 2 the same way and partially open.
j. Put the sets together in an open edge to edge and hinge tape the opposite joining. Notice as the set of 4 is moved the points will form a square pattern and the taped edges are in half an octahedron pattern.

k. This is a top view of a 4 unit section looking down into the long inside of the open tetrahedra.
l. Make 3 of these sections and put them together hinge taping the long edges between each of the sections.

top view

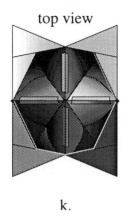

k.

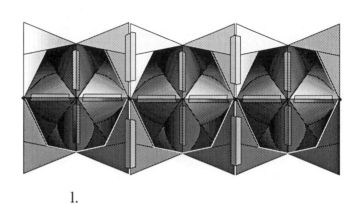

l.

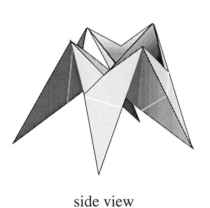

side view

Tape full length of long edges on both sides.

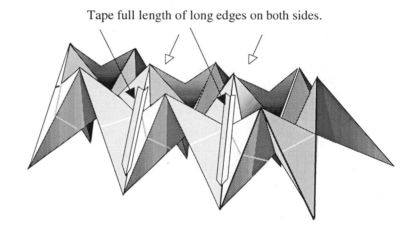

m. When folding the right-angle, triangular sides will always end up surface to surface with each other in the collapsed position. It forms a <u>bi-pyramid hexagon</u> pattern.
n. When turned inside out, it will take a triangular form.

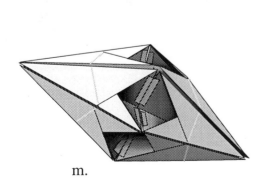

m.

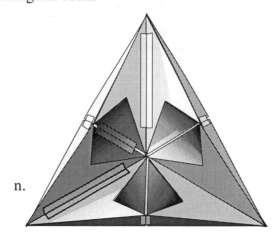

n.

Variations on octahedron movement system

Here are 2 variations in the system of 12 irregular right-angle tetrahedral units. Each different way of hinge joining them together will reveal different relationships resulting from different movement paths. Three sections of 4 units are shown. Adding more sections will extend the movements and complexities of forms.

a. Make the 4 unit section in (3FA-32j).
b. Move the section into the collased form.
c. Put 3 sections into a circle where they share a center point.
   Tape them with a hinge joint on the long edges.
d. Rearrange the three sections into a triangular 'in-out' pattern and tape on the long edges with hinge joints.
   The hinge taping needs to be strong to explore the many positions of these systems.

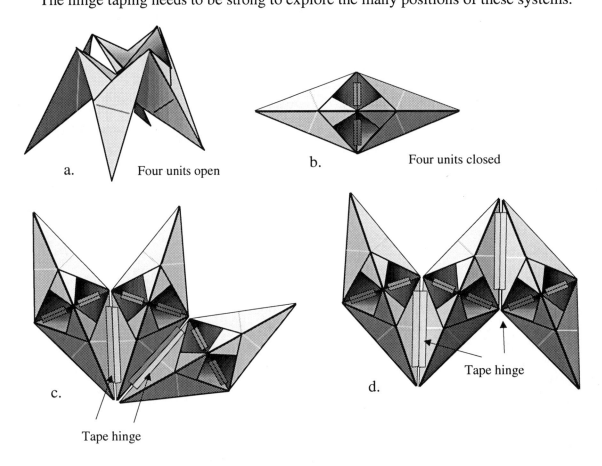

a. Four units open
b. Four units closed
c. Tape hinge
d. Tape hinge

Abriviated octahedron movement system

a. Use the right-angle irregular tetrahedron (3FA-32).
b. Put 4 of them together joining on the short edge of the right-triangles using a hinge joint.
c. Make 2 sections the same way and join them on the points of the long ends. Tape across the 4 joints and press tape around so that there is enough movement and strength to collapse it in both directions.
d. This is the collapsed form. It forms this in 2 directions each through a right-angle movement to the other. The movement collapses the 2 diangonals of the quadrilateral opening.

a.

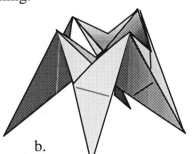
b.

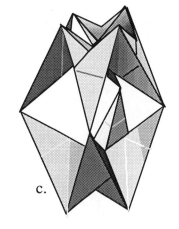
c.

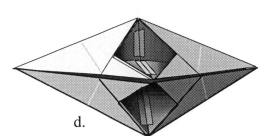
d.

Irregular star

a. Start by making an irregular tetrahedron (3FA-32).
b. Join 4 of them with hinge joints as shown in the octahedral transforming system.
c. Join 2 sets of 4 together by opening them in half and putting the open in-out edges of one into the open in-out edges of the other. There will be 8 long points of the tetrahedra that will form the pattern of a square anti-prism.

a.

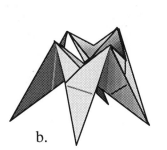
b.

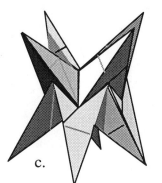
c.

Irregular octahedron movement system

This folding is slighly different than what is shown in (3FA-32). While it looks similar, it is a 4 sided rather than a 3 sided configured unit. Joined into a system it moves through similar patterns but reforms in different ways.

a. Fold the hexagon pattern by folding in the large triangle and fold over 4 of the 6 hexagon sides leaving 2 unfolded on one of the triangle sides.
b. Fold over the triangle side that has the 2/6 sides unfolded. This forms an irregular pentagon shape.
c. Fold on the center line bringing the 2 top edges together.
d. Tape the edges. (It has small curved flaps inside. Glue can be added before the flaps are taped together to give it more strength.)

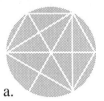 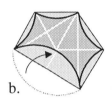 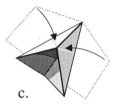

a. b. c. d.

e. Notice in this completed unit 2 right-angle triangles, 2 isosceles and 2 differently proportioned triangular openings. When folded flat one way it forms the large equilateral triangle; flat out the other way shows 5 right-angle triangles.

e.

f. Take 2 of these units and hinge join right-angle triangles together face to face, taping across short edges. Fold units around, edges coming together and tape on other side.
g. Make 2 of these sets of 2 and join them together in the same way as each of the individual units were joined.

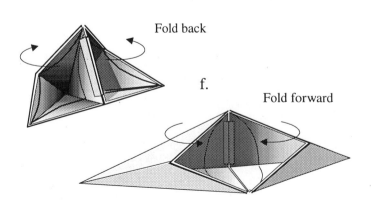 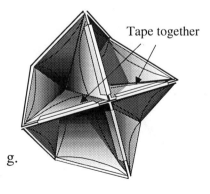

Here are a couple of the coherent configurations this system will move through and some flat shapes that it will now fold down into.

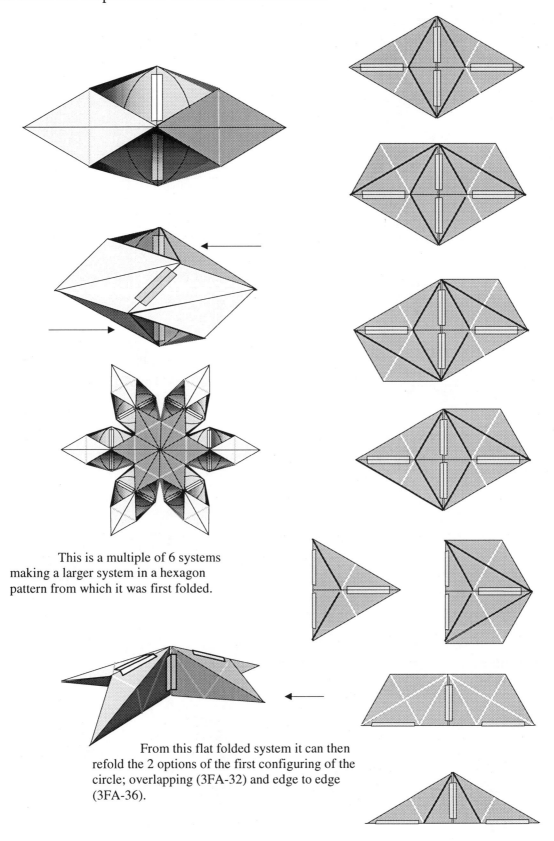

This is a multiple of 6 systems making a larger system in a hexagon pattern from which it was first folded.

From this flat folded system it can then refold the 2 options of the first configuring of the circle; overlapping (3FA-32) and edge to edge (3FA-36).

Reforming the tetrahedron

We shall explore some of the many ways to refold the tetrahedron into a variety of curved forms where the edges are on the outside. It is important to look for the symmetry in the folding patterns.

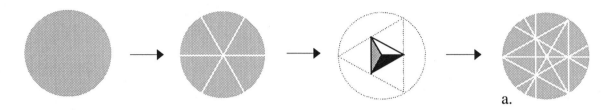

a.

❶ a. Start by folding the tetrahedron (3FA-8). Open it out flat and look at all the folded lines. There are many configurations that can be formed: using only those lines. Notice there are 3 individual systems of folded lines; 1) the 3 diameters; 2) 3 lines forming the large equilateral triangle; and 3) the 3 lines dividing the large triangle into 4 smaller equilateral triangles.

b. Fold one half of triangular prism as shown in (3FA-71two).
c. Fold the curved sections on top flat onto the base triangle.

d. Fold both sides towards the center; bring curved edges together.

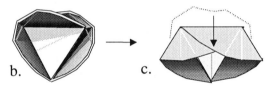
b.   c.

d.

b. Tape the edges together. Here are both the top and side views. Adding glue before taping makes the unit stronger.

e.

❷ a. Identify 2/3 of the large triangle.
b. Push in on the line bisecting the left hand 1/3 part.
c. Continue to fold in and push the 2 end points of the triangle together.
d. Fold the right 1/3 over and flatten onto the left part.

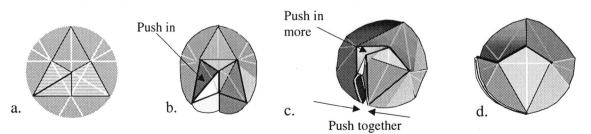
a.   b. Push in   c. Push in more / Push together   d.

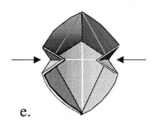  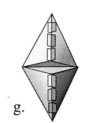 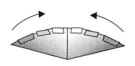

e. f. g. h.

e. Push in mid points from each side.
f. Bring bottom curved edges together and tape.
g. Bring top curved edges together and tape.
h. Side view of figure (g). The 2 parts are hinged and can move to change angulation and relationship between them.

❸
a. Start with open tetrahedron.
b. Fold in one side of the large equilaterial triangle.

c. Fold the 2 corner points together and tape.
d. Fold top of large triangle forward forming a tetrahedron with 2 curved flaps out.

 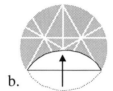

a. b.

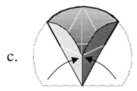 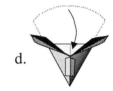

c. d.

e. Fold the 2 curved edges together and tape closed with flaps taped down in back.

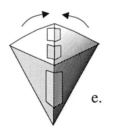 

e. Tape down

❹
a. Starting with (3c) above, fold the triangle all the way back, rather than forward as shown in (3d).

b. Tape the curved edges together and the sides of curved edges to the triangular sides. Front and side views.

 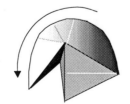 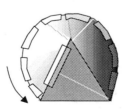

95

5
  a. Start with fold shown in (3c).
  b. Fold along the long bisector pushing sides together.
  c. Fold the bottom curved edges together and tape as shown in (2g).
  d. Tape the top curved lines together.
  e. Push in to change.
  f. Push in to change.

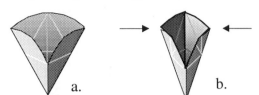
 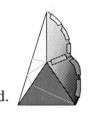 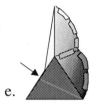 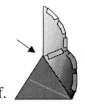

6
  a. Fold on one diameter bringing two curved edges together. Tape up to the <u>first</u> creased line.
  b. Fold the lower curved edges one onto the other. Tape lower curved edges.
  c. Side view of folding.

  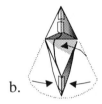 

7
  a. Start with (6a) above. This time tape down to the <u>second</u> folded line. These lines will come to the center of the circle.
  b. Push in/up the end of the diameter to meet the center forming a large triangle.
  c. Fold 2 ends of the triangle together and tape on curved edges.
     This form moves from flat to a right-angle configuration, changing angulation at the same time changing its width of opening.

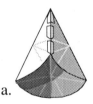 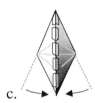 

8
  a. Start with (6a) again. Continue taping to the <u>third</u> creased line.
  b. Pull in bottom triangle making a flap inside and tape.
  c. Bring together curved edges on each side and tape.
  d. Push in on the first folded diameter to reform.

 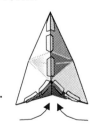  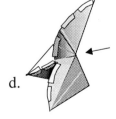

9 a. Start with open tetrahedron.
b. Fold on bottom of large triangle.
c. Bring the 2 end points together.
d. Tape the edges closed.
e. Tape the curved edges together and then tape them to the tetrahedron part.

a.
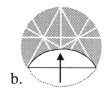
b.

c.
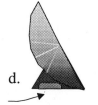
d.

e.

f. Four units of (e) are arranged in a tetrahedron pattern. Fold 2 units of (2h) as shown and add them to the tetrahedral unit just made.

 X 4 = 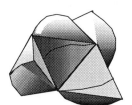 + 2  =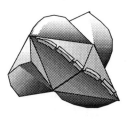

10 a. Join the triangle faces of 2 units (2h) together so that they form an interval congruent to the triangle faces. Join 2 units of 2 in a tetrahedral pattern.

 +  = 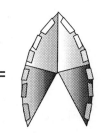   times two is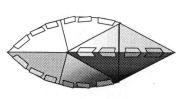

b. Using the (4b) unit to itself in rotated positions will form a spiral.

Half moon tetrahedron

a. Start by folding a tetrahedron (3FA-8). Open the tetrahedron out flat and look at the folded lines. Look for the large triangle and the 3 bisecting diameters.
Fold 2 sides of the large triangle to the back.

b. Find the diameter. Fold segment from point to center towards you; the segment from the center to the line of the large triangle fold in, and the top segment fold forward.

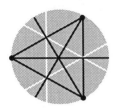 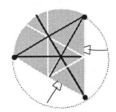  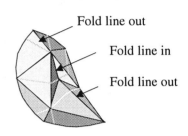

Fold line out
Fold line in
Fold line out

c. Push the 2 corners of the middle triangle towards each other until the 2 halves of the circumference touch each other. Tape the edges together. You might want to put some glue on the edges before taping.

d. Fold 2 units exactly the same. Position one opposite to the other and join along two of the straight edges of each one. It will be clear how they fit.

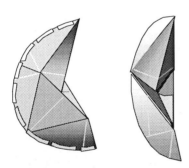 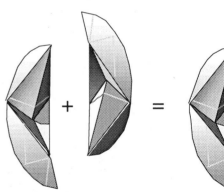

e. Make 2 sets of 2. Look for the quadrilateral openings formed on each set. Join them, opening to opening each at right-angle to each other. It forms a tetrahedral pattern.

 +  =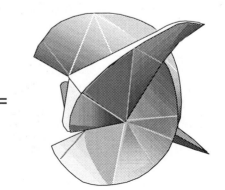

f. Again take the same 2 sets of 2 units and join them together on congruent edges of the quadrilateral opening where the curved surfaces of each come together.

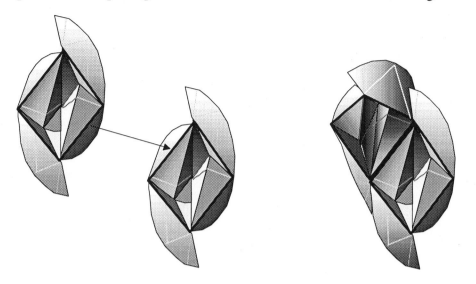

Do this process again joining in the same way. It will begin to form into a spiral. Continue this process and a spiral will develop where all the curved edges are on the outside and the straight edges are on the inside.

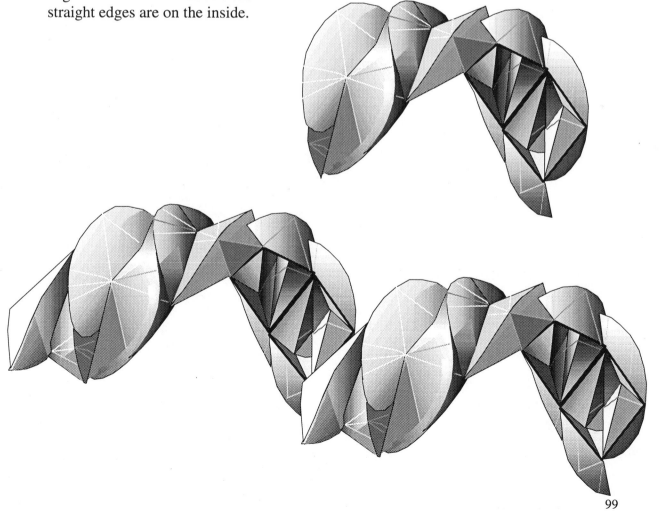

4 -Frequency diameter circle

There are a couple of approaches to folding the three 2-frequency diameters into 4 equal divisions. The first is strongly recommended. It is consistent to the circle form. The others are shown because they do occur. A particular sequence of folding is sometimes an individual preference for what makes sense to the person folding. Each different way of folding is instructive to this process.

1.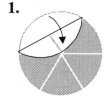

a. Start with the 3 folded diameter circle. The 6 points on the circumference each have a relationship to the center point. Show each relationship sequentially around the circle by touching diameter end points to the center point and creasing well, one at a time. <u>Do not overlap folds</u>: you will lose accurate and parts of the lines will not get folded. Each end point of the 3 diameters to the center forms the hexagon star.

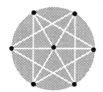 → 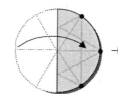 → 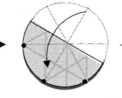 → 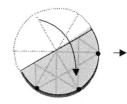 →

b. The opposite ends of the 3 diameters must be folded together enable to complete the 4-frequency grid pattern. Fold an end of one diameter to the opposite end and crease. Fold each of the 3 diameters in this way. This generates 3 more diameters at right-angles to the first 3. They are called bisecting diameters and fall on the intersection between the 2 large triangles that form the hexagon star. They divide the circle into 12 equal sections. The division of segments of the bisecting diameters are not equal, as are the star point diameters. This is the complete 4-frequency diameter folded circle. It shows the relationship of all 7 points to each other.

In drawing a circle, constructing the hexagon and connecting all the points you would get the hexagon star, an incomplete grid. It will be missing the 3 bisecting diameters. It would show only 30 of the possible 42 relationships between the 7 points.

2. The second way seems a clumsy method of folding but makes the process clear.
  a. Start with one of the 3 folded diameters and fold the opposite end points together.
  b. Then fold each end point to the center point.
  c. The diameter is now divided by 3 parallel lines into 4 equal parts.
  d. Do that to each of the other 2 diameters in the same way. This is now the completed grid and shows all the relationships between 7 points.

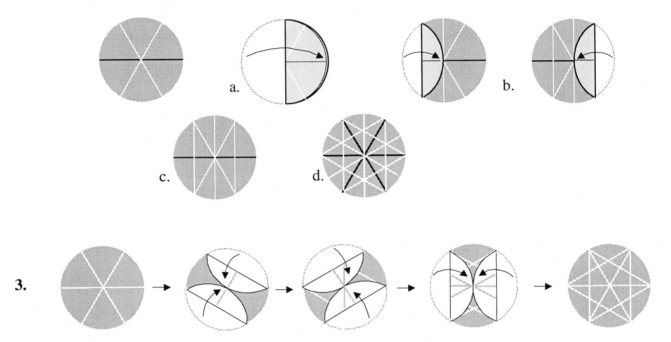

3.

Start with the 3-diameter circle. The 2 end points of each diameter are folded to the center point. Three pairs of parallel folded lines are folded to form the hexagon star. Folding the 3 diameters in half will complete the grid.

4.

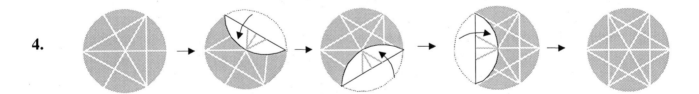

Start with the folded equilateral triangle (3FA-4). Fold individual triangle end points to the center point, crease, open flat, fold the next until all 3 are folded separately. The corner points of the first triangle are the information for the opposite triangle. Fold diameters to finish folding the grid.

There is much information to be discussed when reflecting on the folded 4-frequency diameter circle. This may come at any time after students have become familiar with the folding. Sometimes it is appropriate to save the reflection process until after students have had a time to explore the reconfiguring of the folded lines. It is often important that students get extended experience in folding before they can think about what they've done.

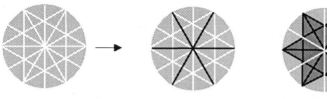

Color in the star. There are 2 sets of 3 diameters. Locate the 3 bisecting diameters half way between the star points. They define 6 rhomboids or diamond shapes, half of them form the hexagon, the other half the star.

The 3 diameters of the hexagon star are the foundation for the development of the triangular grid. To lose them is to become confused.

Lay out the circles the students have colored on the floor and see what happens when lined up on the diameters. This is an extension of suggested activities following folding and ordering the VE sphere (3FA-3). Notice the hexagon diameters remain inside the circles. The bisecting diameters extend outside the circles through the intervals forming unseen hexagons.

Each point tangent point extends the diameters from circle to circle increasing the frequency of the grid. This is the same process as dividing into a single circle. The <u>fractal</u> nature of the equilateral triangle within the wholeness of the circle and sphere is a self-saming pattern generating self-similar functions of form variations.

Color different designs using the folded lines of the grid. Explore the variety of complex shapes and design that can be formed from this pattern.

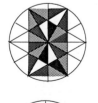 

The squares and pentagons are already patterned into the grid. They are formed by connecting various points of intersection.

Hexagon disk

  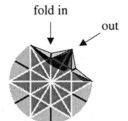  

a. Fold the circle into the 4-frequency diameter grid. Trace in color 2 triangles forming the hexagon star, making it easy to see. Between each star point is a folded line that bisects the angle where the 2 large triangles intersect. Push in each of the bisecting lines up to the point of intersection to form the star points.

b. The crease from circumference to intersection between star points goes in, the star points out. *The only two ways to fold a creased line are in and out.* Fold 2 circles in the same in-out pattern. The star point triangles of one hexagon fit into the spaces between the star points of the other. This is the same process in using 2 tetrahedra to make an octahedron (3FA-11). Both are the pattern of an antiprism (3FA-75).

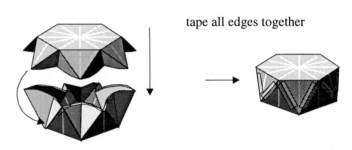

tape all edges together

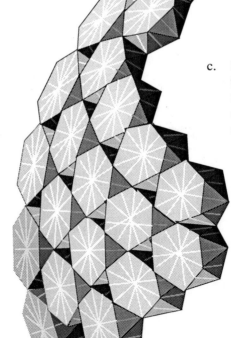

c. How many hexagon disks will it take to make a complete circle? How many to make a full sphere? Will it make a complete sphere? What other forms can be made using these hexagons?

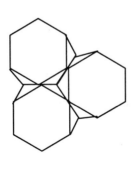

104

Saddle hexagon

The hexagon reflects the flat nature the circle.

a. When 3 star points are folded with edges together, the curved edges inside will not let the triangles lay flat against the hexagon. They make an open pentagon form.
b. Fold the opposite 3 together in the same way. Notice how 2 sets of 3 triangle star points each form an open quadrilateral space. The 2 pentagon shapes share the quadrilateral space. The opposite side is in a curved saddle shape.
c. Push the sides in until the open space becomes 2 equilateral triangles forming 2 octahedra sharing a common triangular side, 9 points in space.

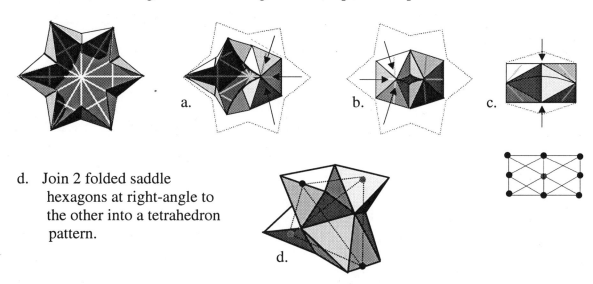

d. Join 2 folded saddle hexagons at right-angle to the other into a tetrahedron pattern.

There are a number of ways to now connect this tetrahedron-patterned form to itself continuing the tetrahedron pattern.

e. This is one way to join 2 tetrahedron units together in a tetrahedron pattern formed as a spatial interval. Use a hinge joint, it will be stronger as you put it together.
f. Join 2 sets of 2 from (e) together, completing the tetrahedron where the spatial interval is now formed in the center of the system.

This form shows perpendicular crossing of 2 opposite edges of the tetrahedron pattern.

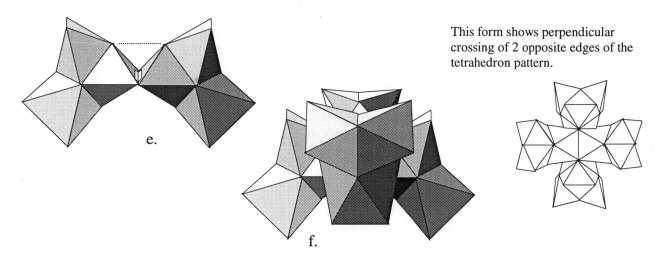

105

Pentagon cone

Fold in 1/6 of the circle pushing in on the bisector diameter between 2 star points. Bring the star points together and tape the flap in back forming a pentagon cone.

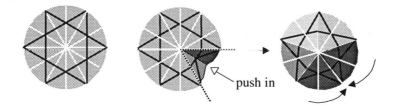

Bi-pentacap

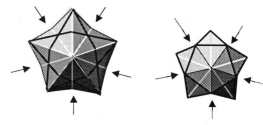

a. Start with the pentagon cone.
b. Push in all 5 creased lines between the 5 star points from circumference to the point of star intersection.
c. This will straighten edges of inside pentagon forming 10 triangular planes, 5 triangles off each edge of the pentagon.
d. Keep folding the 5 triangles back to the other side at the same time pushing the lines between the star points inside. When the 5 triangle points come together, tape along the 5 edge joints.

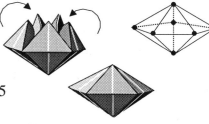

Icosahedron

Start with 2 untaped folded bi-pentacaps.

a. Open the triangles half way, forming a pattern of 5 triangular intervals.
b. Put them together so that the triangles of one fit into the spaces of the other, with all edges touching (3FA-11).
c. Tape along the edges. This is an <u>icosahedron</u>, one of the Five Platonic Solids.

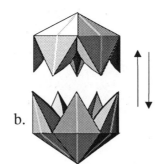

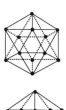

a.   b.   c.

Have students count points, triangular surfaces, and edges of the icosahedron. Identify the middle band, sometimes called the "belly band," with a pentacap on the top, and the bottom. That middle band is an antiprism pattern of alternate positioned triangles.

The grid folds allow the icosahedron to collapse, which is not evident in the traditional solid form of the icosahedron. The collapsing and expanding movement is a function of the right-angle triangle division of the 20 equilateral triangles.

Push in on all creased lines between the edges. It will collapse like an accordion. Push on top and bottom of diamonds to pop it back out.

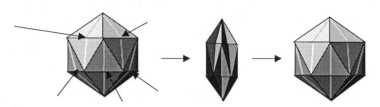

Convex dodecahedron

The <u>dodecahedron</u> is 12 pentagons in a spherical pattern. Make 12 bi-pentacaps and join them together pentagon edge to pentagon edge. The correct angle is inherent in the relationship between edges as they fit together.

   a.  b.  c.

a. Put 2 together and tape edges.
b. Angle them so the edges will line up with the edges of the 3rd bi-pentacap. Tape the edges on the inside and out side for better strength.
c. These 3 will determine the angles necessary to add the 9 remaining bi-pentacaps. Add one on each side making a set of 6. Make 2 sets of 6 and tape them together.
d. This is the full dodecahedron sphere. The fold lines connecting the 12 center points of the pentacaps reveal an icosahedron pattern. The icosahedron and dodecahedron are parts of the same 5-10 pattern. They can be formed individual having inverse symmetries of number of center points and number of sides with the same number of edges. They are called duel polyhedra (p. 33).

d.

Concave dodecahedron

Start with a folded pentagon cone. It will be reformed making a concave pentacap unit that will in multiples be assembled in the same manner as the convex dodecahedron.

a. Begin with the pentagon cone, concave side facing up, point facing down.

a.   Inside of cone.

b. Push the curved edges down around the outside of the center pentagon cone.

b.

c. Fold outside triangle over to the back of the center cone. Tuck in between star points and fold over triangle, tuck in, and fold over and repeat all the way around, then tape.

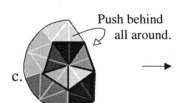

Push behind all around.

c.

d. This forms a pentagon pyramid with the star points folded flat to the outside of the open pentacap.

d.

e. Make 12 open pentacap pyramids and join them pentagon edge to pentagon edge with the open side out, point going in, forming a <u>dodecahedron</u> sphere with concave surfaces.

one open pentacap   two   three   twelve

The single unit of the convex dodecahedron will fit into the open pentacap of the concave dodecahedron providing a way of joining them together. The icosahedron (3FA-44) also fits the concave pentacap.

Icosahedron/dodecahedron system

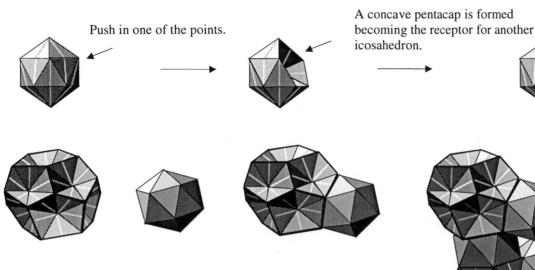

Push in one of the points.

A concave pentacap is formed becoming the receptor for another icosahedron.

The triangular faces of the pentagons are congruent; they all come from the same diameter circle folded from the hexagon grid. They all fit together allowing for development of many designs and different systems. Convex and concave pentagon shapes fit into each other where there is reasonable accuracy in folding the units. The bellyband of 10 triangles is an important connective unit in this building system.

The different patterns of symmetry (the 3, 4, and 5) are interconnected through the proportional relationship of triangles from the same grid matrix.

Make a concave dodecahedron and place an icosahedron in each pentagon depression, expanding the form of the dodecahedron into a more complex form of an icosahedron pattern.

Expanded Dodecahedron

a. To make this dodecahedron begin with the curved edge of the pentacap folded in the direction of the convex cone.

b. Trace the lines of the pentagon star with a marker so you don't lose track when joining folded circles. The pentagon is pointing to the outside.

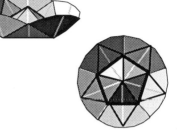

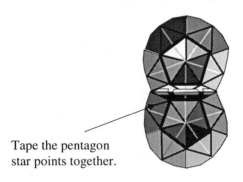

Tape the pentagon star points together.

c. Join 2 by putting a star point from each one together (tape on the star points with curved flaps together). <u>The lines between the star points will form a triangle corner of 3 pentagons coming together.</u>

d. Add a third circle, taping star points together. This brings the 3 circles to a triangular intersection.

Tape 2 circles together on curved edges close to triangle joining.

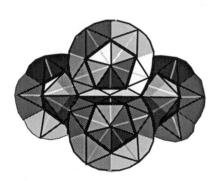

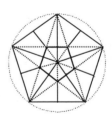

e. Four pentagon circles joined on their curved flaps show the line symmetry observed in the completed dodecahedron patterned sphere.

f. Here there are 6 pentagon circles-1/2 spherical dodecahedron, all joined on the curved flaps as shown above. Two sets of 6 circles taped together makes the full pattern of 12 circles.

Within the pattern of the pentagon lies the proportional 5-10 division that forms both the icosahedron and dodecahedron.

Stellated dodecahedron

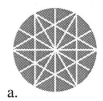
a.

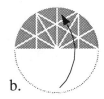
b.

c.

d.

e.

a. Start with the 4-frequency diameter circle.
b. Fold in half, 6/12 of the circle is showing.
c. Move the ends around to form a 6-sided cone.
d. Overlap 1/6 of the circle forming a 5-sided cone. Tape along the over-lapping edge. This open pentagon pyramid has congruent edges to the dodecahedron (3FA-46).

e. Fold the curved edges to the inside from point to point, making a straight edge to the pentagon. (You can fold these curves in while the circle is still flat by folding the hexagon sides between each star point.)

f. Make 12, 5-sided pyramids, and put one on each pentagon face of the dodecahedron. This is traditionally the stellating process of extending the center point of a plane above the surface. It is only one form of in-to and out-from movement of the center of spherical pattern.

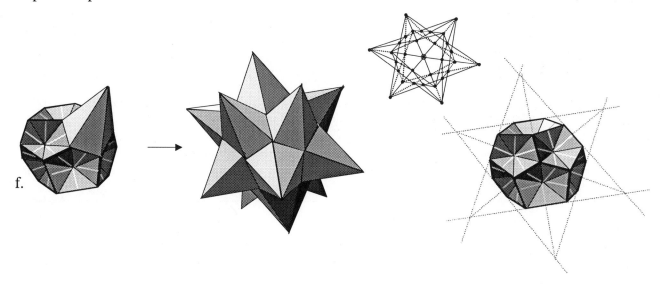

f.

Have students do a perspective drawing of what their models looks like, and then a drawing that shows the proportionally patterns of the underlying organization.

Extended tetrahedron

Stellation is the movement of the center point of a polygon extending perpendicularly above the plane. This forms a cone if the plane is a circle and a pyramid when the plane is a polygon. This movement extends the polygon back into a volumetric form. Every point in the circle grid functions as a center point. This provides a wide range of proportional options for stellated polygons. Folding the tetrahedron is the simplest way of making a stellated triangular plane (3FA-8).

Start with a circle folded to the hexagon star pattern. For this folding it is unnecessary to include the three bisecting diameters of the grid.

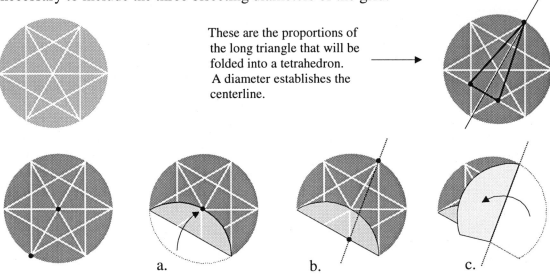

These are the proportions of the long triangle that will be folded into a tetrahedron. A diameter establishes the centerline.

a. Fold the star point to the center point on the crease already there.
b. On the base line locate one of the points of intersection and the opposite star point on the centerline.
c. Fold a line connecting those 2 points.

To facilitate accurate folding of long lines, place a metal straight edge or ruler between the 2 points and fold the paper over, then crease well.

d.

e.

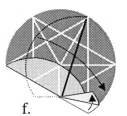
f.

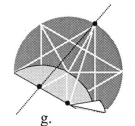
g.

d. Fold the part extending beyond the bottom edge under and make a strong crease.
e. Make sure the crease is in line with the bottom edge.
f. Fold large flap out and fold small flap on top using the crease folded in steps (d) and (e).
g. Repeat steps (c) (d) (e) and (f) on the left hand side in the same way.

h. These are the folds you should have so far. Look for the symmetry of them.

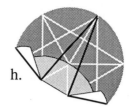

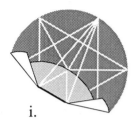 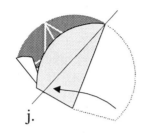 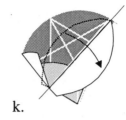 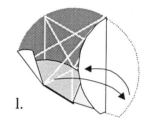

i. The space between the 2 small folded flaps is the base line of the triangle.
j. Fold large flap over to match triangle base using the first fold of the triangle long edge.
k. Fold curved edge back from end point of the triangle base, on the long edge of triangle.
l. Open both new folds out and fold over last fold from (k) in the other direction, re-crease it.

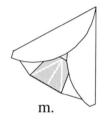 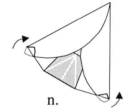 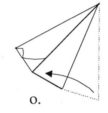 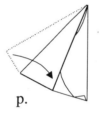 

m. Repeat sequence of folds (j, k and l) for the left side.
n. Fold the small overhangs up so both sides of base line are straight.
o. Re-crease the long side of the triangle to get a sharp line.
p. Re-crease the other long side of the triangle.
q. Fold the 2 long edges together and tape them closed.

❶ Square base pyramid

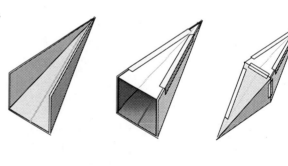

Leave (q). from above untaped; open it to form a square interval. Make another the same and join them to form a square base, tape together. Tape together on open ends for bi-pyramid.

❷ Pentagon base pyramid

 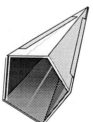 

Open the square interval to a pentagon. Add a second folded circle, overlapping one side, completing the last 2 sides of the pyramid and tape. Tape together on open ends for bi-pyramid.

Great stellated dodecahedron

Fold an icosahedron (3FA-44). Make an extended tetrahedron (3FA-50q). Attach the open end of the long tetrahedra to one of the faces of the icosahedron.

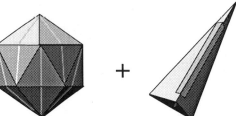 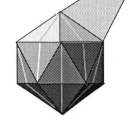

a. Make 3 more long tetrahedra and place them on the icosahedron with the first in regular intervals where the points form a tetrahedron pattern.
b. Make 4 more long tetrahedra and place them onto the icosahedron with the first 4 where all 8 points form a cube pattern.
c. Make 12 more and finish taping them to the rest of the triangle faces on the icosahedron making it fully stellated with the points forming a dodecahedron pattern.

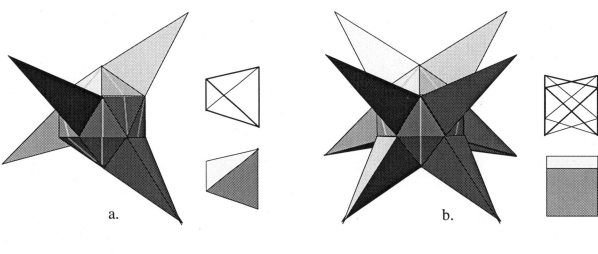

Within the 5-fold symmetry of the icosahedron is held the tetrahedron, the cube and dodecahedron with the octahedron evident as 6 edges in the cubic form. The stellation of the icosahedron shows the interconnection of all the 5 regular polyhedra in pattern.

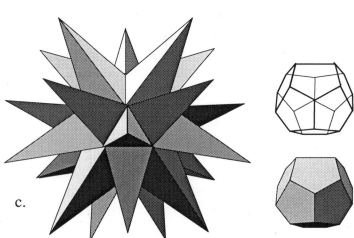

Extended tetrahedron variations

Fold the circle as shown in extended tetrahedron (3FA-50), but leave out in step (n), don't fold the small tabs over.

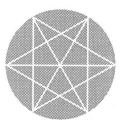

Fold steps (a-q) leaving out (n).
Open circle and fold base line of triangle. ⟹

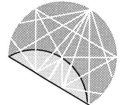

Here are 15 folded variations using combinations of lines and points of intersections reforming the same extended triangle base.
There are more, plus hundreds of combinations.

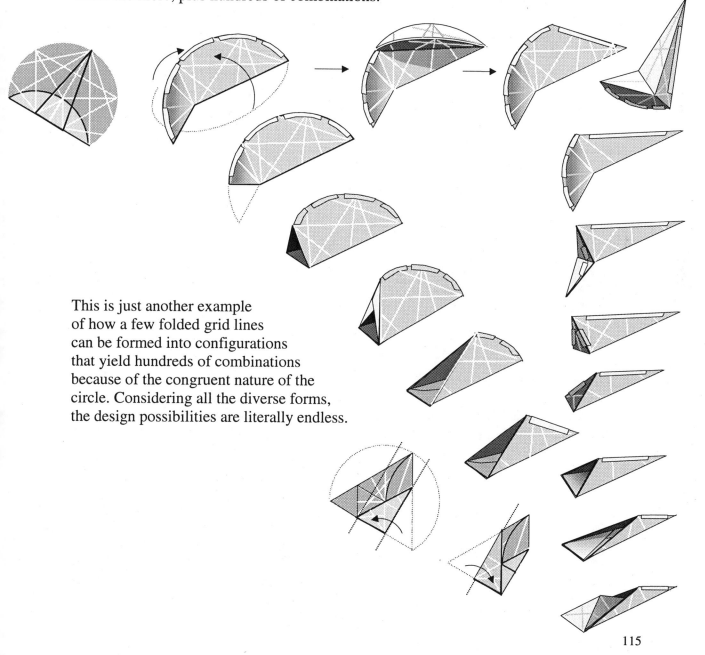

This is just another example
of how a few folded grid lines
can be formed into configurations
that yield hundreds of combinations
because of the congruent nature of the
circle. Considering all the diverse forms,
the design possibilities are literally endless.

Small octahedron

 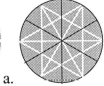 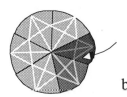 

a.   b.   c.

a. Start with the 4-frequency diameter circle. Identify the 3 bisecting diameters.
b. Fold in 2/6 of the circle on the bisector between the star points forming a square pattern.
c. Fold the 2/6 flap flat against the inside wall of the cone and tape it down so it does not get in the way while folding.
d. Push in the lines between the star points. This forms 4 triangles, one on each side of the center square. This is the same process shown in formimg pentacap (3FA-42)
e. Put the end points of opposite triangles together.
f. Push flaps down making 2 flat triangles. This will close the top of the octahedron. This is a useful configuration for other systems
g. Fold triangle flaps up onto the sides of the octahedron.
h. Tape the edges holding the octahedron together.

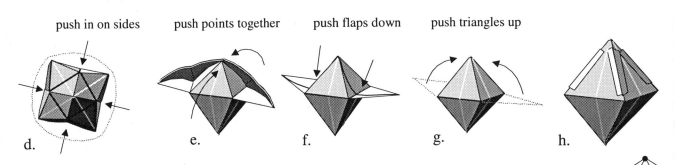

16 side deltahedron

Start with the folded octahedron. Do not tape. Open it half way, forming triangle intervals. Do 2 of these the same way. Put individual triangles of each into the intervals of the other and tape the edges together.

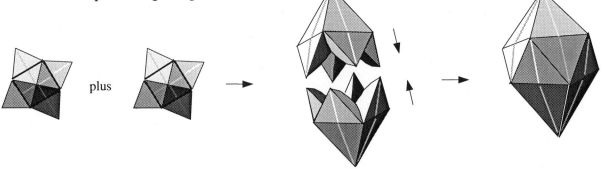

40 side triangular pattern

A. Start by folding a 4-frequency diameter circle, folding it in half, on one of the bisecting diameters, so you can see the ½ hexagon. Bring the radii of the folded diameter around and join together with a bobby pin or tape at the same time pushing in on the half hexagon lines. That will bring up the center to a 3 sided point, forming a triangular hat.

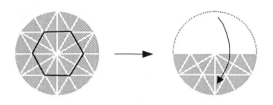
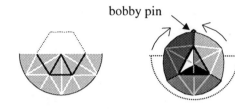

This time make 4 of these units and attach them together at the star points in a tetrahedron pattern. Put 3 on the bottom and one on top.

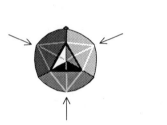
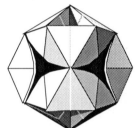

Notice the curved edges form a triangular opening in a hexagon shape. There are 4 hexagon sides where each of the triangular planes is in a different agnulation, not all laying on the same plane.

B. Fold 4 more 4-fequency circles and fold into a large triangle. Then form the hexagon shape by folding in the 3 corner triangles.

Tape all edges down

Alternately fold each radial line; one up, one down all around causing a depression in the center.

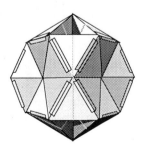

Tape each folded hexagon onto each of the 4 hexagon sides as they fit to the slightly in-out alternate folds. The 4 open tetrahedra could be closed making a "solid" (enclosed) polyhedron by cutting the folded edges and allowing the 3 triangles to fold up to form a flat plane across the triangular openings. I do not suggest cutting the circle and there is no reason for making it a "solid" figure.

Some form variations to this pattern are folding the concave tetrahedron out instead of in; or put the hexagon sides pushing out rather than in. Fold it from 8-frequency circles enable to truncate in combinations.

C. Here an interesting pattern is revealed. When 4 of these units are put together in a tetrahedron pattern they form the octahedron interval that is exactly the shape of the unit itself. That means that 5 of these forms will fit each other to make a complete tetrahedron pattern. That is exactly what we see when 4 sets of 4 spheres forming tetrahedra into a tetrahedron pattern, a space created that will except another set of 4 making 5 sets in a tetrahedron pattern instead of 4 as seen in regular polyhedral form.

Three views of this tetrahedron pattern.

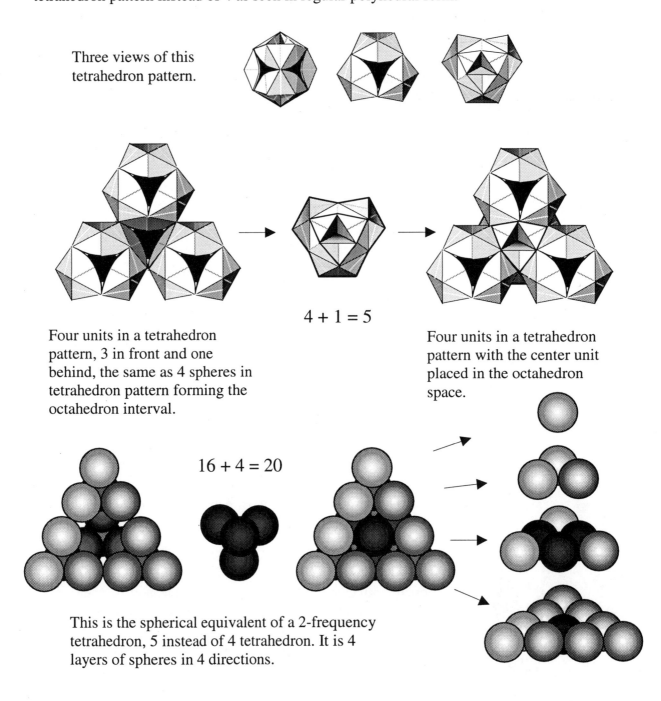

4 + 1 = 5

Four units in a tetrahedron pattern, 3 in front and one behind, the same as 4 spheres in tetrahedron pattern forming the octahedron interval.

Four units in a tetrahedron pattern with the center unit placed in the octahedron space.

16 + 4 = 20

This is the spherical equivalent of a 2-frequency tetrahedron, 5 instead of 4 tetrahedron. It is 4 layers of spheres in 4 directions.

D. Make a tetrahedral system as shown in (A). Make 4 more individual hat units. Put a single unit into the hexagon side of the system corresponding to the point where the 4 are put together.

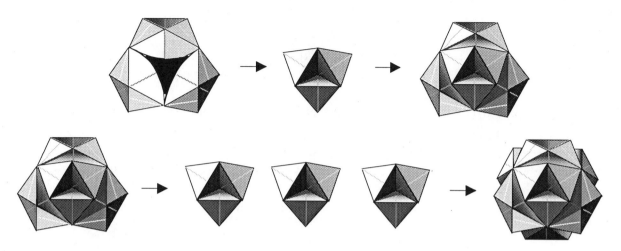

Continue to place three more triangular hats in the same way on the other 3 hexagon sides of the system.

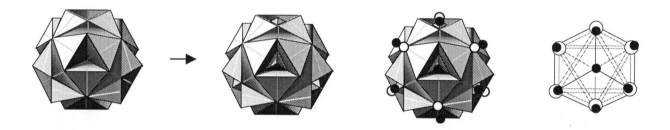

The pattern of this spherical form is both the octahedron and cube. The center of the triangles (black) show the 8 points of the cube; the octahedron is a pattern of the 6 points (white). When the image is drawn the hexagon pattern is revealed. By stellating the triangular planes the corners of the cube become clear. Eight individual tetrahedra can be added, or you can start with the unit where the tetrahedron goes out instead of in.

Octahedra can be added where the triangles are congruent. Here we can see a wonderful fractal growth mechanism where the form is being modified and the pattern remains consistence.

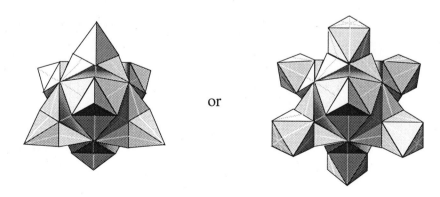

119

Inside out octahedron

Fold the octahedron (3FA-11).
a. Open the top 4 points and pull out between opposite star points making 2 large flaps. Tape flaps together on the curved edges.
b. From the open position push in one end of flap, forming a concave triangular space making the third side of the top half of the octahedron. Bring together curved edges and tape as before.
c. Before taping (b) push in the other side the same making another concave triangular space on the opposite side forming the last side of the octahedron. Tuck in and tape the curved edges together as before.
d. Before taping the last curve of (c) fold the 2 curved flaps over flat on to the triangle side of the octahedron leaving one curved section out.
e. Fold curved edges over into a hat like form. Bring curved edge together and tape the same as in (a) above.

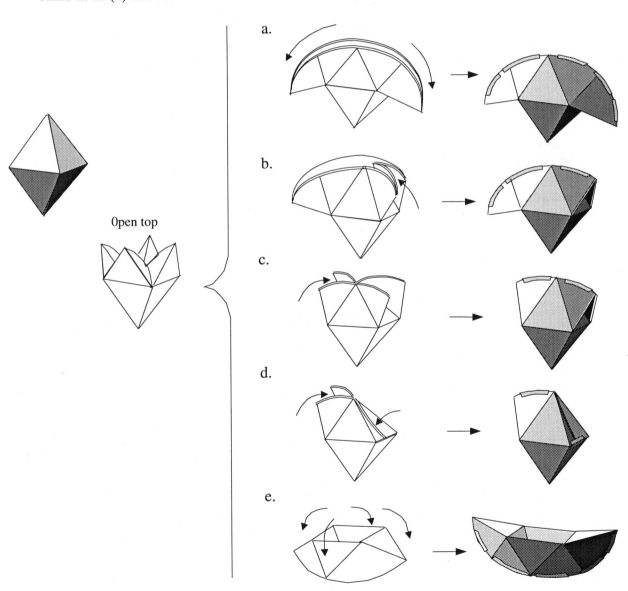

Octahedral spiral

a. Reform the octahedron with 3/4 of the curved edge out (3FA-56b).
b. Make 13 similar. Reduce the diameter of the circle as each successive unit is folded in the same way. Start out with about 3/8-inch reduction and adjust proportional as you fold smaller.

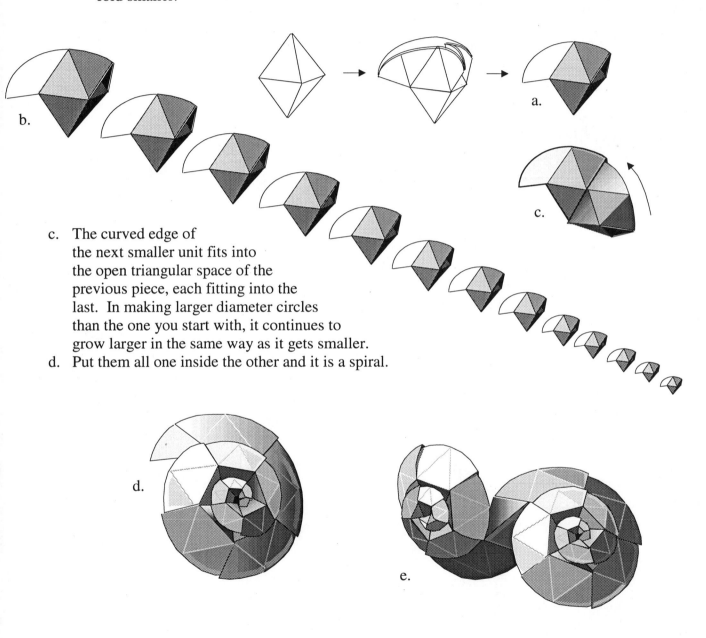

c. The curved edge of the next smaller unit fits into the open triangular space of the previous piece, each fitting into the last. In making larger diameter circles than the one you start with, it continues to grow larger in the same way as it gets smaller.
d. Put them all one inside the other and it is a spiral.

e. A double spiral can be made by using a tetrahedron to join them together. The spiral can be made right or left-handed and can be joined the same or in opposites.

121

Winged octahedron

Fold the octahedron and leave the triangular flaps out (3FA-53f). There are many advantages to leaving the triangles out. They allow for attaching and developing systems that otherwise would be difficult. This will be explored along the way.

 ## Winged half octahedron

There are 2 variations in forming the half octahedron with triangular flaps.

1. Folding half octahedron with curves inside.

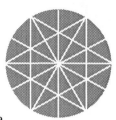 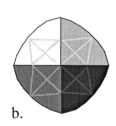 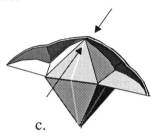 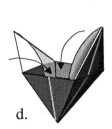

a.   b.   c.   d.

a. Start with a 4-folded grid.
b. Fold in 2/6 forming the square.
c. Push 2 opposite star points towards each other forming the bottom half.
d. Push both top points into the bottom half pressing the triangles against the inside walls.
e. Flatten 2 remaining flaps out.
f. Option: fold triangles together completing open octahedron pattern.

2. Folding half octahedron with curves outside.

 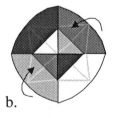 

a.   b.   c.   d.   e.

a. Start with the folded square.
b. Fold the circumference up around the center pyramid.
c. Fold the 2 opposite star points to the pyramid point.
d. Push the curved edges on one side down onto pyramid side.
e. Push curved edges on other side onto the edges just folded.
f. Turn over with triangles flattened out.
g. Option: fold triangles down on to sides forming a square pyramid.

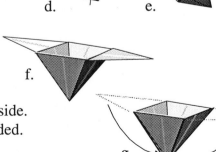

Small rhombicosidodecahedron

Start with 5 units of half an octahedron with triangle flaps.

Put the triangle ends of each unit together, edge to edge forming a pentagon and tape where they join. The pentagon can be formed in or out. For this model, the pentagon cones will be concave.

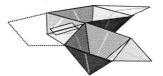

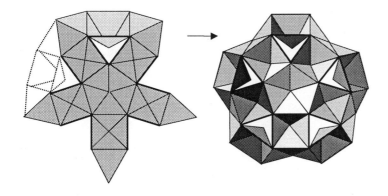
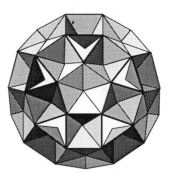

Put 5 more units between each of the first 5 so that the 3 squares form 5 open triangular intervals around the pentagon hubs.

Continue this process putting all the triangular flaps into pentagons. As you do this with all 30 units it will form a sphere in the icosahedron pattern.

This same unit can be used to make the sphere with the pentagons protruding out or in, the square pyramid in or out, or as the full octahedron with triangle flaps. Each variation will change the form of the sphere using the same unit in the same spherical pattern. Below are the 3, 4, and 5 symmetry of this system. The small rhombicosidodecahedron is unique in that it demonstrates the triangle, the square, and the pentagon with all sides congruent.

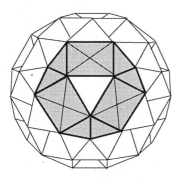
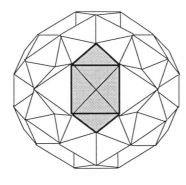
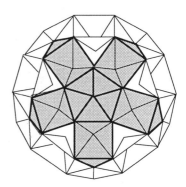

three units   one unit   five units

123

VE tetrahedron

Here we will explore the development of the winged half octahedron with curves outside. Other variations can be introduced in many interesting ways. Those will not be addressed here, but are open for discovery.

a. Fold the unit as shown (3FA-59,2f). It will take 6 folded units.

b. Take 3 units and join them in tetrahedron pattern, pyramid points to the center, joining pyramid edge to pyramid edge. Use bobby pins to hold edges together. Tape or glue, then remove bobby pins.

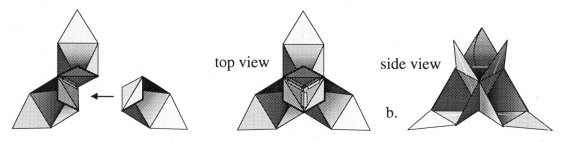

c. Add one more unit to the above set of 3. Place it to complete one of the 3 tetrahedral intervals.

d. Add the last 2 units in the remaining tetrahedral intervals completing the vector equilibrium pattern of alternating triangles and squares.

e. Bring the edges of the triangles at the open ends together forming ends of tetrahedron. Lay end flaps flat to form the vector equilibrium.

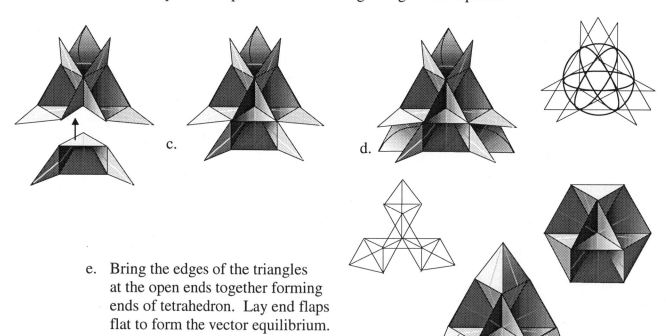

VE tetrahedron system

a. Use the open end VE Tetrahedron (3FA-61d). Two of them will join together at the open ends. It is the same as putting 2 individual tetrahedra together forming an octahedron (3FA-11).

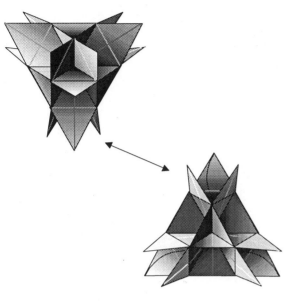

b. This is the double unit.

c. Three sets of the double unit will go together in the same way. It is the same hexagon pattern that is found in the Benzene Matrix (3FA-89). When the form of a pattern is changed it often will generate greater complexity.

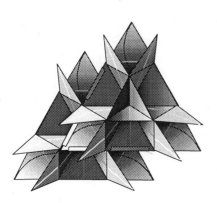

d. There are other ways these units will go together. Explore them.

Stellated octahedron

Start with the 4-frequency diameter circle. Fold one of the large equilateral triangles.

 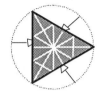

fold 3 curved edges behind

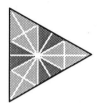

Fold in from the center point on the crease dividing the dark triangle. Do the same to all 3 triangles. This will raise the center of the circle into the end point of a tetrahedron.

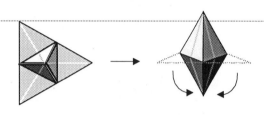

Fold the triangle flaps down bringing the points and edges together opposite the first formed tetrahedron. This forms 2 tetrahedra joined by a surface plane, a bi-pyramid tetrahedron.

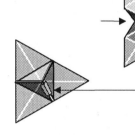

Tape along the 3 edges as they form the tetrahedron on the flat triangle.

Fold 4 circles as above. Put them together in a tetrahedron pattern joining and taping along the edges of the large equilateral triangles. This forms the cubic pattern of the stellated octahedron (3FA-15).

 ## One half tetrahedron

Fold the 4-frequency diameter circle.
a. Fold end points of one diameter on any 2 parallel lines to the circle center point.
b. Fold 2 corner points of one edge to the center point using the folded lines.
c. Fold it in half with the shorter side lining up with the longer parallel side.
d. Open out the folded sides half way.
e. Fold up the 2 end triangles so the edges come together forming a square opening. This forms 1/2 of a 2-frequency tetrahedron.

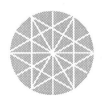 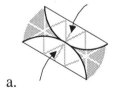 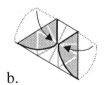   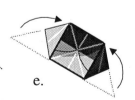

a.   b.   c.   d.   e.

This configuration is one half of an octahedron and 2 tetrahedra.

Here are a couple of things that can be done with the one half tetrahedron.

1. **Tetrahedron puzzle.**

   Fold 2 one half tetrahedra and try to join them together to form a complete tetrahedron. While it is very simple it usually takes a little while. There seems to be a tendency to put faces together in parallel rather than at right-angles.

   Two units joined on the square faces at right-angles to each other will form the tetrahedron. Together they reveal the tetrahedral pattern of 10 points in space showing clearly the square as it lies in both the octahedron and tetrahedron.

2. **Vector equilibrium puzzle**

   Make 4 half tetrahedra and join them in alternate square and triangle pattern.

   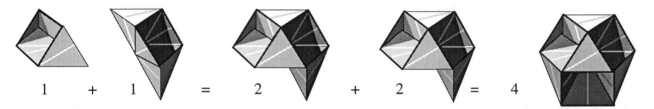

3. **Hinged tetrahedra.**

   Push the diagonal points of the square opening together. As the square collapses the tetrahedra become closed and hinged to each other.

4. **Forming a tetrahedron/octahedron all-space filling system**

   The half-tetrahedron form and the small octahedron (3FA-53) together can be arranged leaving no space between them. There are many designs and combinations of varied complexities of spatial intervals to be explored.

   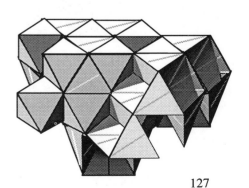

Four triangles form a tetrahedron

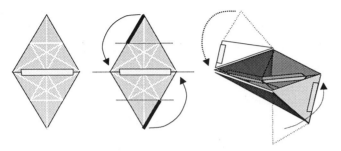 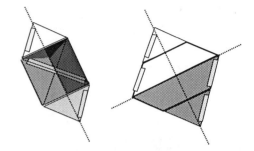

a. Join and tape 2 folded triangles.
b. Fold the opposite edges on top and bottom to adjacent sides and tape.

c. Square the open rhomboid.
d. Put 2 formed units together; square onto square intervals perpendicular to each other forming a large tetrahedron. (1FA-64l)

 Four triangles form a tetrastar

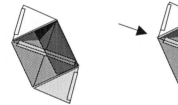 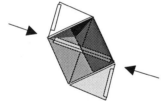 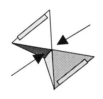 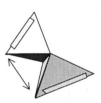

a. Fold 2 units as shown above (3FA-65c).
b. Push opposite corners of the squares together. This forms 2 tetrahedron joined by the taped edges that join the 2 large triangles.
c. Push tetrahedra of each set together until the space forms a regular tetrahedral interval between the individual tetrahedra.

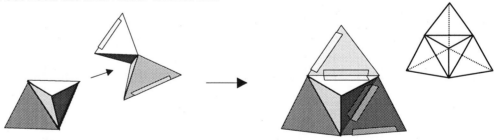

d. Form 2 the same way, putting the triangles into the triangular spaces of each other. Tape the edges together. This forms a stellated tetrahedron; a polyhedron with 12 equilateral triangles.

Tetrahedron/octahedron combination

 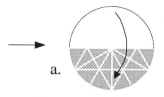  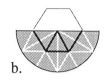

angle of the pentacap

angle of the octahedron

angle of the tetrahedron

a. Fold a 4-frequency grid circle on one of the bisecting diameters.

b. Look for the half-hexagon around the center. Push the center up and the half-hexagon folds down until there is a hat-like pentagon, a square, and tetrahedron as the two halves of the diameter are pulled together. Pin edges closed with a bobby pin.

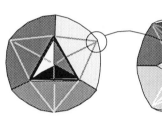  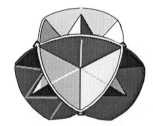 

c. A single tetrahedron. Notice the 6 star points are now 3.

d. Two units joined, with a bobby pin at the star points with tetrahedron joined on an edge.

e. Three units joined at star points with edges joined together, using 3 bobby pins.

f. The forth unit joined at the star points, with all tetrahedron edges together. The 6 bobby pins create a lot of tension. They are the 6 points of the octahedron. The 4 points form the tetrahedron pattern.

Three views of the tetrahedron/octahedron combination form. The line images of the pattern from each view shows the unseen center tetrahedral interval.

 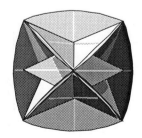 

Six petal tetrahedron/octahedron

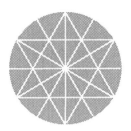 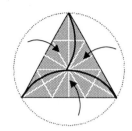  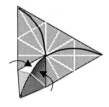

a. Start with the 4-frequency grid and fold the large equilateral triangle.

b. Open up 2 curved edges that go from the center to one of the end points.

c. Bring the curved edges together and tape. Use 4 or 5 short pieces of tape rather than one long piece.

 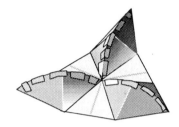

d. Fold all 3 corners with curves coming together.

e. Tape along the curved edges to hold closed. A little glue along the edges before taping will make it stronger and last longer.

 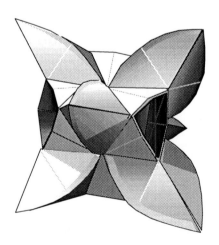

f. Join 3 folded units by putting the triangle faces together so the curved edges form petal shapes and the straight edges of the hexagons form a triangle space. Tape along the joined edges.

g. Tape the fourth folded circle, triangle faces to the remaining triangular faces completing the tetrahedron pattern in an octahedron form.

Folded petal

a. Fold and tape the 3 petal triangle (3FA-68e).

b. Push in the triangles between the petals on the center crease.

c. Tape the 3 triangles in half; bring the petals together.

d. Make 2 petal units and hinge tape them together on the edges of the petals. As a single movement system of 2 units there are difference positions to explore.

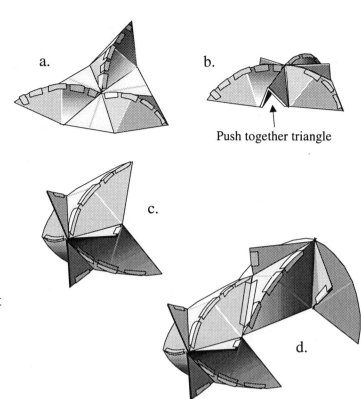

Truncated petals

a. Fold the 4-frequency grid.

b. Push in star points leaving bisector diameters out, folding on the hexagon.

c. Fold the star points flat onto the circle with 6 curved flaps standing up.

d. Fold the curved flaps together in 3 sets of 2 where the curved edges are taped together.

e. Fold the triangle between curved sets in half and tape closed. Again there are different configurations to explore.

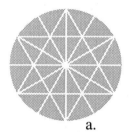
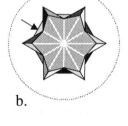

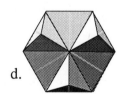

Equilateral triangular prism

A prism is a polyhedron with 2 opposite sides congruent and parallel, separated by parallelogram shaped planes.

ONE

a. Start with a 4-frequency grid. (3FA-39) Find the centered hexagon and the 3 diagonal that will form one of its triangles.

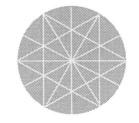 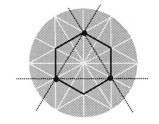

b. Locate 3 lines on the circumference, each parallel to the lines that form the center triangle, every other hexagon interval from star point to star point. Fold them over.

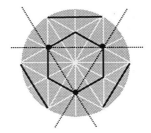 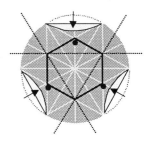

c. Fold between the triangle points, a line parallel to the lines just folded on circumference.

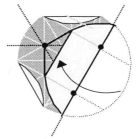 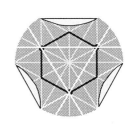

d. Look for lines in triangles between rectangles off each edge of the center triangle. Fold in the center line bringing the rectangle edges together. This forms the triangle prism. Tape edges.

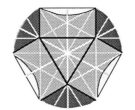 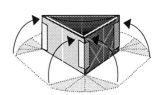

e. This prism pattern is not a solid form. It has one base plane open. It can be closed by folding a flat triangle and taping it on top. Two or more can be taped together extending the length.

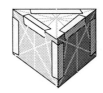

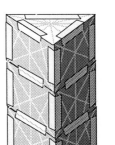

TWO

Here is another way to fold the triangular prism.

a. Fold the tetrahedron and open out flat (3FA-8). Fold over along the base line that defines the small center triangle.

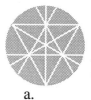 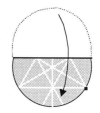
a.

b. Fold lower right corner of large triangle to point on top opposite side. Leave curves open.

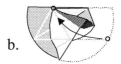 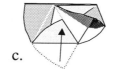 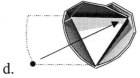
b. c. d.

c. Fold over on base line of triangle, lining up with left side of triangle. Keep it flat.

d. Fold lower left corner over to opposite point on the upper right, leaving curved sides open.

 + =
e.

e. This makes a triangular-type cup. Tape the 2 overlapping sides holding it together. Make another the same way, put open end of one into the open end of the other.

3FA 72 Right angle triangle prism

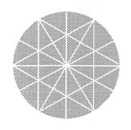 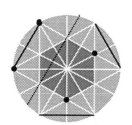 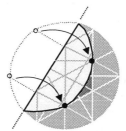 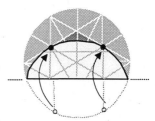 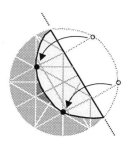

a. Fold a 4-frequency grid. Find the line interval between star points parallel to 2 of the diagonals of the hexagon. Alternately there are 3 sets of 4 points.
b. Fold one diagonal hexagon line by touching the 2 points on the circumference with the 2 corner points on the opposite side of the hexagon. Do the same thing with all 3 sets of double star points. Open the circle and look for the 2 parallel lines at right-angle to the lines just folded. They are the lines of the opposite sides of the hexagon. Those 4 lines form a rectangle.

f. Locate points on the circumference; the end points of the lines that bisect the left side and base line of the triangle just folded in steps (b and c).
g. Fold each of those points to the first point of intersection on that line which will be 3 corner points of the hexagon.

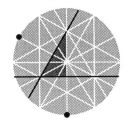 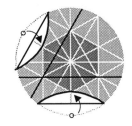

h. The lines just folded are parallel to the edges of the triangle diagonals.
i. Fold the 2 star points on the top of the circle down to the corners of the hexagon that lie on the same line.

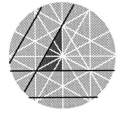 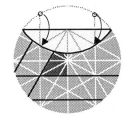

j. Open flap and look at the new folded lines. Notice the parallelograms that extend off each edge length of the right-angle triangle.
k. Looking at the right-angle triangle, locate these 2 points that when connected by a fold line will bisect the right-angle. Fold that line.

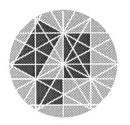 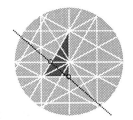

l. Locate 2 more points, one just formed by the last fold and the other, the top point of the right-triangle. Fold a line between them.
m. This is the unfolded right-angle triangular prism.

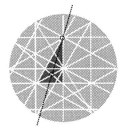 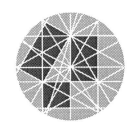

n. Fold under on the outside line on each of the 3 parallelograms.
o. Fold in on the bisecting lines of the 3 intervals between the parallelograms. This will fold the edges of sides of the prism together.

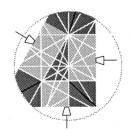 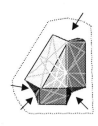

p. Tape along edges. It has an open bottom.
q. Make a right-hand and left-hand prism that together form an equilateral triangular prism.

134

Square prism

The cube is a square prism with 3 sets of parallel planes. These are only a couple of ways to form the cube pattern (3FA-94) (4FA-6) (4FA-18,21) (5FA-9m). Rectangular prisms are inherent in the cube by extension and parallel division.

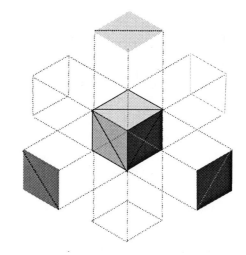

Pentagon prism

a. Fold an octahedron (3FA-53).

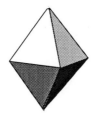

b. Fold one half of the octahedron into the other half forming a square based pyramid (3FA-59).

c. Put the 5 half-octahedron units into a pentagon pattern with open square planes to the outside, points to the center (3FA-77a).

 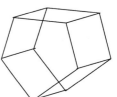

d. This is a pentagon prism pattern. It fits the outside description, but it does not look like a prism form. The prism form made only with outside shapes has no structural stability; no triangles to hold its shapes. In the folded model, both the square and the pentagon openings are relationship formed by triangles.

Antiprism

The antiprism differs from the prism in that the 2 bases are rotated to each other half the distance of the edge length. This divides each quadrilateral side of the prism into 2 equal triangles.

1. Triangle antiprism

The triangle antiprism is the octahedron. The formation of the octahedron pattern comes from the 2-frequency division of any kind of triangle. Halfway closed from triangle to tetrahedron is the triangle antiprism. The intervals are congruent to the triangles that make them. (3FA-11)

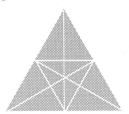 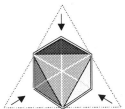

2. Square antiprism

The <u>square</u> antiprism is a 10-sided polyhedron.
a. Fold a 2-frequency 4/8 grid (4FA-5) and fold to a square.
b. Fold corners of the square down forming smaller square.
c. Make 2 and put them together, triangular flaps edge to edge, and tape.

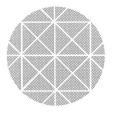   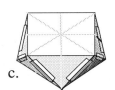

a. b. c.

3. Pentagon antiprism

a. Fold a 5/10-grid (5FA-7).
b. Push in creases forming the large pentagon star (5FA-8).
c. Fold star points down until they are perpendicular to the pentagon.
d. Put 2 together, star points fitting into each other edge to edge.
e. Tape antiprism edges.

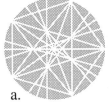 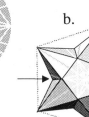  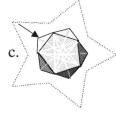 

4 Hexagon antiprism
a. The hexagon antiprism is made by joining 2 hexagon stars folded into each other (1FA-40).

Transformational anti-prism pattern

a. Fold a 4-frequency diameter grid. Fold 2 opposite star points to the center on folded parallel lines.

  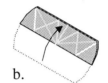

a.   b.

b. Fold in half along the same diameter; this makes a strip of 5 equalateral triangles and 2 curved end shapes.

c. Bring the 2 curved ends around and join to each other lining up the points and straight edges to complete the sixth triangle in an octahedron pattern. Notice the stability.

 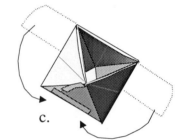

c.

d. Fold and join 2 circles overlapping the curved ends. Fold it around overlapping to form a square.

One of these square prisms will make 2 tetrahedra. Two square prisms will make one tetrahedron.

e. Open up the 4 into 5, forming the pentagon prism pattern. Explore some of the other forms this will make.

This prism will reform into 2 tetrahedra and one octahedron.

f. Add another circle to the strip to make a hexagon and a heptagon antiprism. The more folded triangles there are to the ring, the more transformations it will go through.

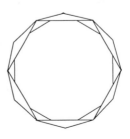

137

Octahedra in pentagon pattern

Often students want to put 5 tetrahedra together to make a pentagon. There is a gap. The angles don't fit. Rather it is the octahedron that has the angles allowing 5 to fit into a pentagon pattern.

Five octahedra form a pentagon star of triangles and squares. The angles of these shapes and intervals provide attachments for the development of many combinations. We will explore some of the variations.

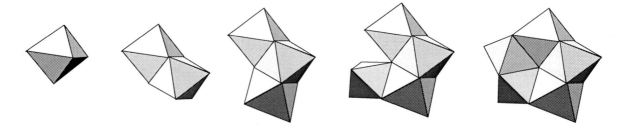

a. Five octahedra form a pentagonal star showing 30 equilateral triangles.

b. By folding half the octahedron inside the other half, a concave square based pyramid is formed (3FA-33). Joining 5 reforms the pentagon star.

  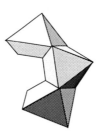  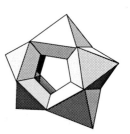

c. By truncating the octahedron the star system changes. Truncation is formed from the 8-frequency folded grid. Putting 5 together with points to the outside will produce a star shape; with points to the center the star will be in a truncated form.

d. Combine (b) and (c) from above; put 5 together to make this form.

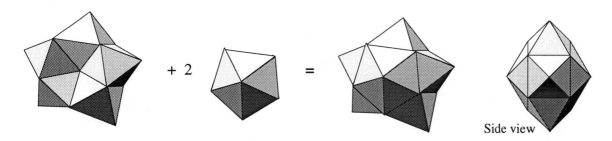

e. Form the pentagon star. Make 2 bi-pentacaps (1FA-43) and put one on each side of the star. This forms a solid star of 10 rhomboids and 10 equilateral triangles. It is 7 circles combining 3, 4 and 5.

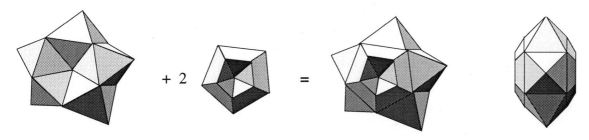

f. Fold the bi-pentacap from an 8-frequency grid forming a pentagonal depression in the center. Tape into the 2 pentagon depressions of the star.

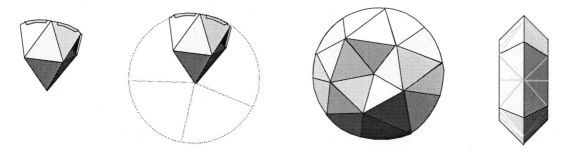

g. Reshape the octahedron as shown (3FA-56c). Put 5 of them into a pentagonal pattern. A variation is to put them in the same pattern at right-angle to the circle.

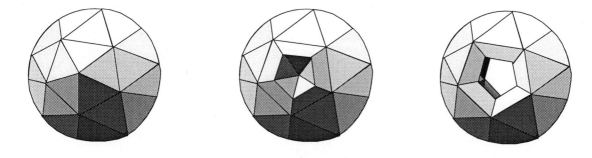

h. Reform the pentagon center by changing the inserts and reforming the octahedral unit to explore different combinations and variations.

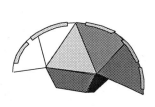
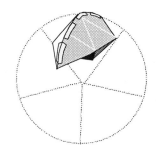
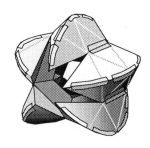

i. Use 5 curved forms of the octahedron (3FA-56a) placed at right-angles to the plane of the pentagon. This is another variation of the pentagon pattern.

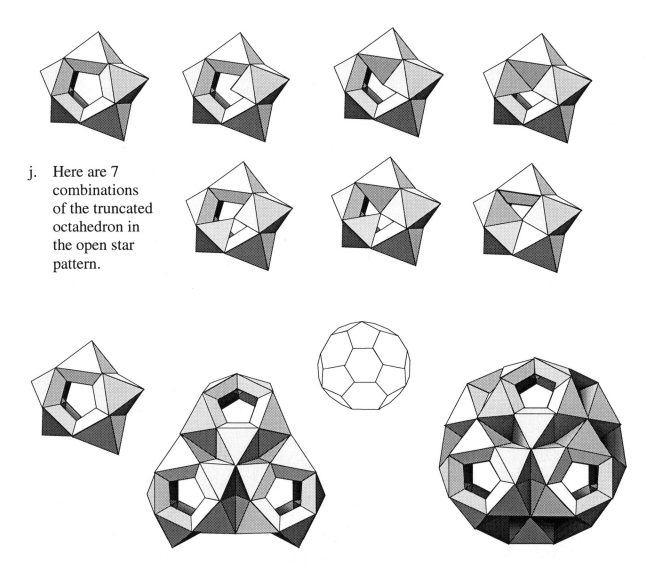

j. Here are 7 combinations of the truncated octahedron in the open star pattern.

k. Using 3 of the pentagon stars (b) form a hexagon pattern.
Six units are joined to form half the truncated icosahedron patterned sphere. Twelve pentagon stars will form the complete spherical pattern (p. 31). This pattern is used in the hexagon/pentagon soccer ball design.

l. Here is another way to form the pentagon star using right-angle tetrahedra. Fold a 4-8 grid and make 5 spheres with the curved edges folded into right-angle tetrahedra (4FA-3). One pentagon star is 20 circles.

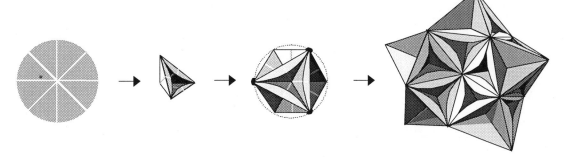

m. A spherical patterned can be formed using 12 stars. It will take 4 right-angle tetrahedra, times 5 octahedra, times 12 pentagon stars, for a total of 240 circles. There are a lot of math questions that can be asked before folding begins. How many will each student have to make? How long will it take? How many bobby pins? How big will it be? Is it worth doing?

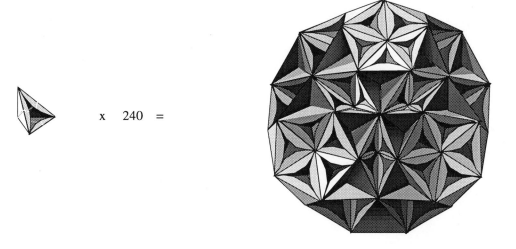

n. This spherical pattern can be taken to much greater levels of complexity by elaborating on the individual units. The units must remain consistent to the initial pattern or development will break down.

141

8-frequency diameter circle

Review folding the 4-frequency diameter grid.

Fold the circle in half. Fold it in a ratio of 1:2 three times generating three 2-frequency diameters. The relationship of 7 points to each other forms a 4-frequency diameter circle grid. Within the 4-frequency grid is revealed all the information necessary to fold the 8-frequency grid.

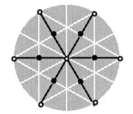 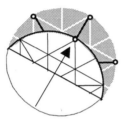 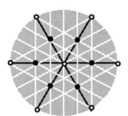 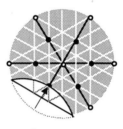 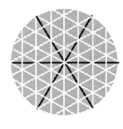

a.　　　　　b.　　　　　c.　　　　　d.　　　　　e.

a. There are now 13 points of intersection that lie on the 3 diameters that formed the hexagon star.
b. Fold each of the star points onto the furthest new point of intersection on each diameter, half-way between the center and opposite end point.
c. This forms two 6-frequency equilateral triangles on the circumference. *As you fold and crease each star point, open it out before doing the next fold.*
d. Fold each star point to the closest new point of intersection on the same diameter line.
e. This is the complete 8-frequency diameter circle grid, much like an octave in music. Each of the 3 diameters of the hexagon pattern is divided into 8 equal sections allowing the development of numerous combinations and spatial overtones. Regardless of the increase of grid frequency, the hexagon-patterned circle of 3 diameters is fundamental to all formation.

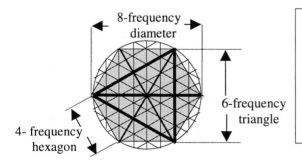

The generative nature of this folded grid pattern is in the right-angle relationship between the equilateral triangular grid and the 3 diameters. This right-angle function is primary to identifying various levels of organization within spherical order. The right-angle is the movement of every fold in the circle, the half-way division perpendicular to the direction of touching between 2 points.

Breaking down the octave process, we can see what happens with the individual diameters. Keep in mind that if we do not start with the whole we miss most of what happens with the parts and will see almost nothing of what is generated between them. *Unity is the nature of the whole, reflected in triangulation that allows endless forming of individual expression throughout.* <u>*Unity does not come from putting parts together*</u>.

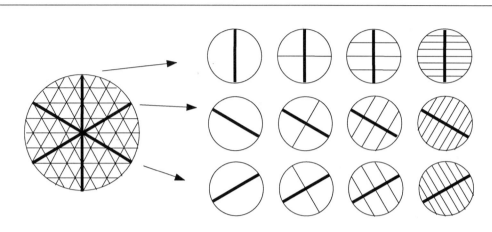

Folding the diameter is the first movement of the circle. Right-angle division is exactly the same for all 3 diameters, each in different orientation. Together they form an organizing refractive grid. The proportional division of 3 diameters in the hexagon pattern is ordered to the nature of the circle. New information is continually generated because each individual part is multi-functional in relationship to each other.

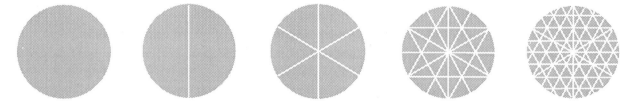

The circle generates a single diameter. Three 2-frequency diameters are generated from that information. From these 7 points 3 diameters are increased to 4-frequency. Following the process the diameters divide into 8-frequency, dividing the circle into an equilateral triangular grid. This self-saming process of developing a higher frequency grid is endless, limited only by the relative scale of the material. *This is a fractal process where pattern absolutely reproduces within the self-similar forming of endless diverse systems.*

Note the 30° shift of the 60° triangle causing a 90° division from 2 to 4-frequency.

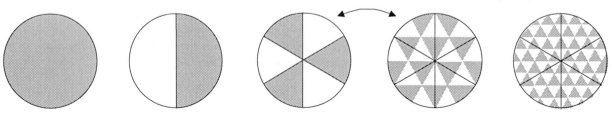

144

Truncated tetrahedron

Start by folding the 8-frequency diameter grid (3FA-78). Fold curved edges under forming the large equilateral triangle. Fold the triangle into the tetrahedron.

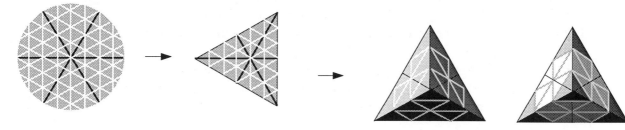

Look for the hexagon pattern on all sides of the tetrahedron and the smaller 4 end tetrahedra, above shown darker than hexagon.

As you fold up the tetrahedron the dark triangles get folded in.

Push 3 triangles in.

tape

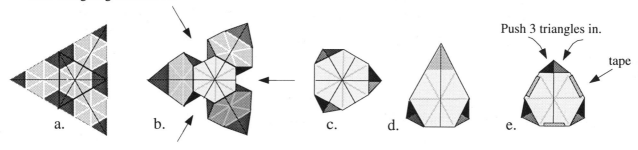

a. Look for the 4 hexagons. They will locate the 3 half-hexagons and 3 triangles corners.
b. Fold in the 3 half hexagon in the middle of each side. They will form a square interval before collapsing into a concave tetrahedron.
c. Three corners inverted, seen from the bottom.
d. Side view of top of tetrahedron.
e. The triangles that make the fourth end point are folded in on the creased lines forming the remaining inverted tetrahedron. Tape the 3 corners where the hexagons join.

Traditionally this is a truncated figure where each corner of a solid tetrahedron is cut off leaving a flat triangle plane (p. 34, 35). This is a truncated tetrahedron pattern of 4 hexagons and 4 inverted tetrahedra, a function of the 3-frequency tetrahedron.

There are a lot of variations that can be formed from the truncated tetrahedron. We will explore some of these further, and how various patterned systems are developed from the angles of these folds.

Variation of truncated tetrahedron

a. Fold the triangle into <u>square intervals</u>.
b. Turn the unit over with the corners pointing up.
c. Fold one corner triangle, 2-frequency, just past the center.
d. Tape both sides to the corresponding edges of square intervals.
e. Fold over the second end triangle, on top of the first, in the same way as the first and tape.
f. Fold the third triangle over on top of the other 2 and tape the edges.
g. Turn over and find the hexagon and square intervals. This is a basic unit with many interesting angles to it.

a.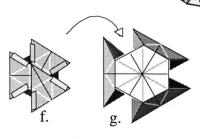

b.

c.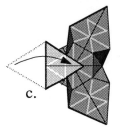

d.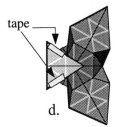

e.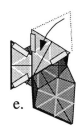

f. g.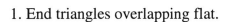

Modifications of variation in the truncated tetrahedron.

1. End triangles overlapping flat.

2. Push the center overlapping triangles in making a concave tetrahedron in the center.

3. Fold the center overlapping triangles out forming a small tetrahedron on top.

There is a correspondence of the angles of the unit to the different patterned systems that it will form; the tetrahedron, the octahedron/cube, and the icosahedron/dodecahedron. The 3 modifications of this unit will, when joined, in multiples, change the look of the system and the means of interlocking.

Variations in tetrahedron pattern

Using a variation of the truncated tetrahedra (3FA-80, 3), put 4 of them into a tetrahedron pattern with the raised center points to the inside. They are joined long edge to long edge. Tape along edges.

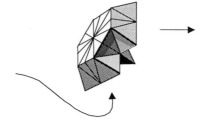

Use the same 4 units with the raised points to the outside and put them in the same tetrahedron pattern as above. This time they join on the middle edge of the square intervals.

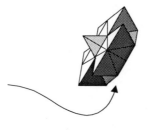

Using the same units again in the tetrahedron pattern, join them on the edge where the edge of the half-hexagons come together, with the interval the space centered to a 2-frequency triangle.

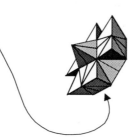

Variation in octahedron pattern

Eight of the same units are joined in an octahedron pattern. They are attached to each other on the 3 sides of the square intervals. The raised center tetrahedron of each unit forms the 8 points of the cube pattern and the square openings form the 6 sides of the cube and showing the 3 perpendicular right-angle axes of the octahedron.

Variation in icosahedron pattern

The angles of the trapezoid planes allow joining 5 of these units into a pentagon pattern. As other units are joined to the pentagon in the same manner, an icosadodecahedron pattern is formed. Twenty identical units are used to form this sphere.

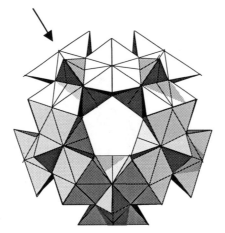
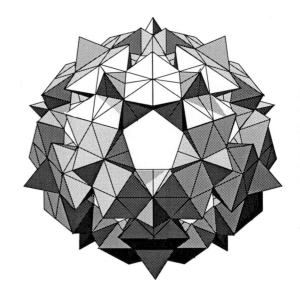

Irregular truncated tetrahedron

a. Fold the triangle, as shown in (3FA-79d), with 3 corners pushed in making a partial truncated tetrahedron.
b. Push in one of the 2-frequency triangles on the top.
c. Push down the next triangle on top.
d. Push down the remaining triangle.
e. This is a modified truncated tetrahedron with a hexagon on one end and an equilateral triangle on the other.
  Anyone of these stages of change can be used to develop systems variations.

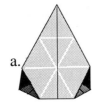 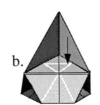 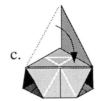

a.   b.   c.   d.   e.

Joining truncated forms

Fold the 3-frequency tetrahedron from the 8-frequency circle grid. Fold the top triangles flat on to each other forming a truncation. Do the same thing two-thirds down the tetrahedron, further truncating.

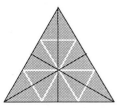 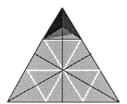 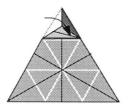 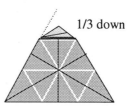 1/3 down 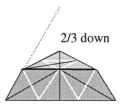 2/3 down

Here are 2 basic ways to join truncated forms; a face to face joining of planes, and opening the corner to form an octahedron joined point. Both ways are strong connections. Joining faces produces the pattern of a prism.
The octahedron connection is an antiprism.

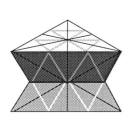 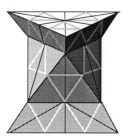 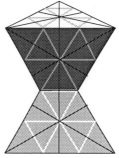 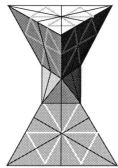

Faces joined.   Open flaps and join making octahedron connection.   Faces joined.   Open flaps and join making octahedron connection.

Footed triangle

a. Fold the triangle into the square intervals (3FA-80a)

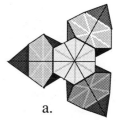

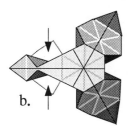 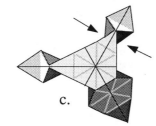 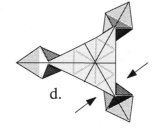

b.   c.   d.   a.

b. Push diameter of hexagon together behind star point diameter. Tape the 2 edges as they touch on other side.
c. Do this the same way to the next triangular arm.
d. Do the same to the third arm to complete the symmetry. There are many different configurations of this design depending on the particular in-out joining of creases.

Footed triangle in hexagon pattern

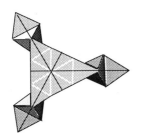

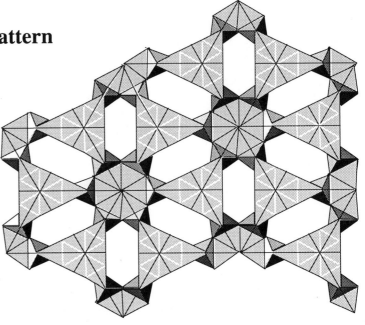

Above are 11 units joined by edges of the corner triangles in a hexagon pattern. The planer nature of the hexagon is evident in the flatness of the design, even though the module is dimensional. By joining the end triangles in pentagons, squares, or triangles the systems become spherical to the 5, 4, or 3 fold symmetries.

Footed triangle in spherical pattern

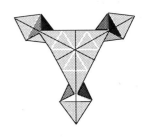

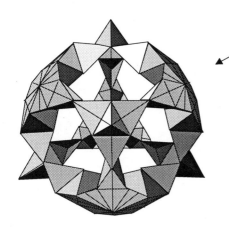

To the left, 4 units are joined in a tetrahedron pattern. The corner triangles are joined edge to edge forming 4 small tetrahedra that are the end points of the tetrahedron pattern. This reveals the octahedron and the cube within the tetrahedron.

It also shows the outside vector equilibrium pattern of 8 triangles and 6 square open spaces without a center.

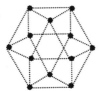

The same triangle ends of the unit that form the hexagon above and the tetrahedra to the left can also be joined into a square pattern of 8, 12, and 20 units. The unit itself can be reconfigured to change the formation of a given pattern.

Benzene ring

a. Fold an 8-frequency diameter circle and configure it into a tetrahedron (3 FA-79). Don't tape it yet.

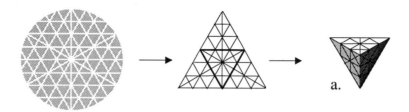

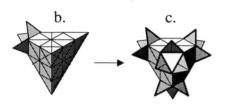

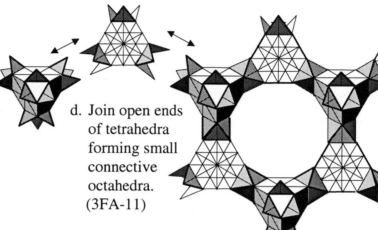

b. Fold back triangles of one corner of tetrahedron.

c. Cut open the other 3 corners with a sharp blade or scissors and fold as with the first corner. Tape the edge where the hexagons join. Each corner is a triangular opening with 3 triangle flaps. *This is one of the few times it is necessary to cut into the circle. Nothing is cut away.*

d. Join open ends of tetrahedra forming small connective octahedra. (3FA-11)

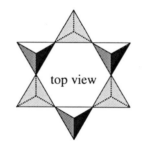
top view

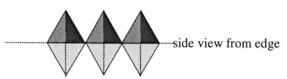
side view from edge

3 tetrahedra, points up and 3 tetrahedra points down. One face of each tetrahedron is sharing the same hexagon star plane.

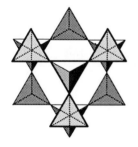 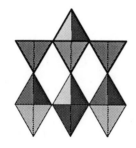

e. Four more tetrahedra are added on top to the ring, joining them in the same way. Stability is in the tetrahedron pattern and octahedra joining. There are now 6 on bottom and 4 on top, 10 tetrahedra in a tetrahedron pattern.

f. Here the 4 open space intervals are shown as a proportional division of a truncated tetrahedron pattern. This space is reflected in the solid form of the truncated tetrahedron (3FA-79e).

Right-angle tetrahedron

a. Folding a regular tetrahedron (3FA-8).
   Open the folded circle out flat, view the folded pattern.

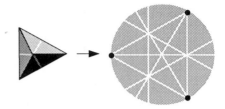

b. There are 6 points on the circumference generated from folding the tetrahedron. They are the end points of 3 chords that form the base triangle for the folded tetrahedron. This center triangle is also the base for the right-angle tetrahedron folding.

These 3 chords are parts of the 8-frequency grid, although the entire grid need not be folded to form the right-angle tetrahedra.

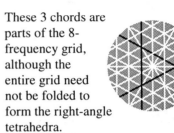

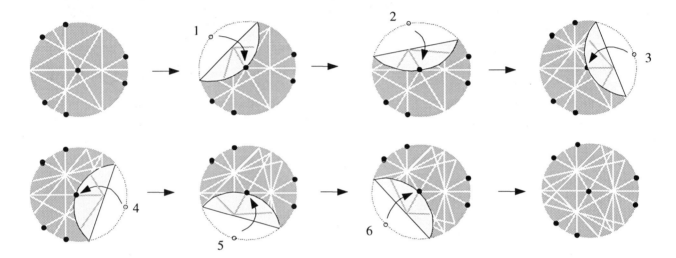

c. Each of the 6 points, the 3 sets of 2 new points on the circumference, has a relationship with the center point. Show each individual relationship, one at a time, by touching each one to the center point and creasing well. They will make 6 new folded lines. Open the circle. Find 2 new equilateral triangles that touch on the circumference.

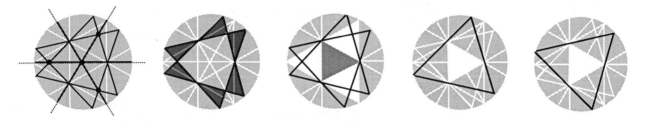

d. The first 2-frequency triangle provides the symmetry for the 2 new equilateral triangles proportionally to the right and to the left. They are congruent to the first and form right-angles where they cross each other on the 3 hexagon diameters.

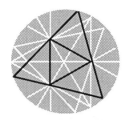 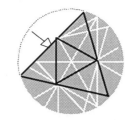 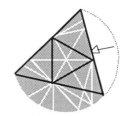 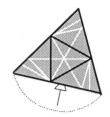

e. Trace out with a marker one of the new off centered triangles and the base triangle from the regular tetrahedron. That will also be the base for the right-angle tetrahedron. Fold under the curved edges on the new creases of the large traced triangle forming the 3 sides of the off-center triangle.

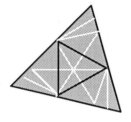  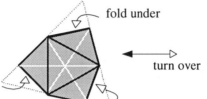

fold under

turn over

f. The curved flaps are on the bottom and the folded lines on top.

g. Notice the right angle triangles on the 3 corners, the 2nd line in from the end points.

h. Fold each right angle triangle behind, making a hexagon shape with 3 right angle corners.

i. Turn the hexagon over with folded right triangles flat on top. Locate the center triangle and fold the large right triangles on each side over and re-crease to get a good sharp edge with the base triangle.

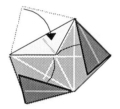  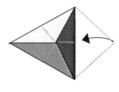

tape edges together

j. Fold the right angle corners up, end points coming together on top forming a right angle tetrahedron. The equilateral triangular face of this right angle tetrahedron is congruent to the regular tetrahedron and the octahedron. It is another component in the spatial "alphabet".

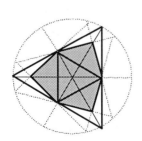

  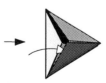

A way to hold the right angle tetrahedron closed without taping is by tucking the flaps into each other.

2-frequency right-angle tetrahedron

Join 4 right-angle tetrahedra touching point to point in a tetrahedron pattern. (3FA-9)

 ## Right-angle octahedron

Join 2 right-angle tetrahedra, each half-open, the sides of one fit into the intervals of the other (3FA-11). Tape the joining edges. This form is the space of the 2-frequency right-angle tetrahedron shown above.

 ## Open right angle octahedron

4 right-angle tetrahedra joined face to face form a half-octahedron pyramid.

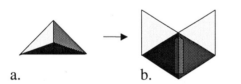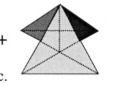

a.   b.   c.

a. Start with one right-angle tetrahedron.
b. Tape 2 together, symmetrically on the short sides.
c. Make another set of 2 in the same way.

d. Put the 2 sets of 2 together in opposite directions so each set of equilateral triangles fills the space of the other making a square on the same plane.

 ## Right-angle tetrahedron cube

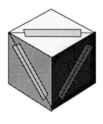

a.   b.   c.   d.

a. One right-angle tetrahedron.
b. Tape 2 together along the long edges.
c. Tape another set of 2 the same way, making 2 sets of 2.
d. Tape the remaining long edges together where the triangles of one fit into the triangle spaces of the other.

Tetrahedral cube development

By using the right-angle tetrahedron to develop cubic pattern some interesting spatial relationships can be observed from different angles of viewing.

a. Pictured are 3 different views of the same tetrahedron pattern of joining 4 cubes edge to edge. Each cube is formed using 4 right-angle tetrahedra.

 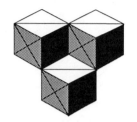 

b. Add 4 right-angle tetrahedra in each interval on (a) touching on end points with right angle corners pointing out. This is in a tetrahedron pattern and completes the edge lines of the cube form.

 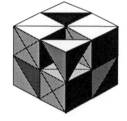 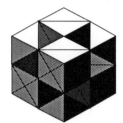

c. Make 3 more of this same cubic unit and put the 4 of them together in the same way. As before, add 4 right-angle tetrahedra to the corners. They will be 2-frequency this time. This makes a larger more complex cube formation.

 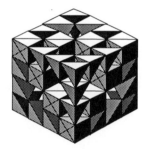 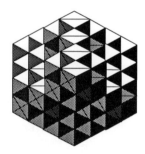

Below a 2-frequency right-angle tetrahedron is placed on each side of a 2-frequency regular tetrahedron. A 2-frequency cube is formed. It much easier to understand spatially than by looking at pictures where all spatial information has been compressed to flat shapes.

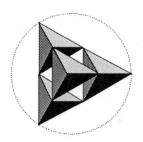 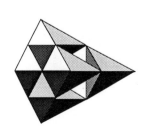 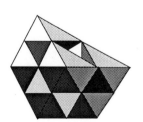 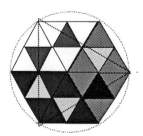

Right-angle tetrahedron-cuboctahedron

Here is another variation on the cube pattern using right-angle tetrahedra.

 a.   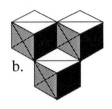 b.   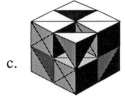 c.    d.

a. Start with a cube made from 4 right-angle tetrahedra.
b. Make 4 and put them into a tetrahedron pattern.
c. Complete cube form by putting in the 4 corner tetrahedra
d. The 4 corner tetrahedra are in a tetrahedron pattern.

e. Put 2 right-angle tetrahedra on one of the 6 of the cube faces. Join them touching on their short edges with right-angle face attached to 1/2 face to the center of each square on the large cube.

f. Put 2 more right-angle tetrahedra on each of the remaining 5 sides of the cube in the same way.

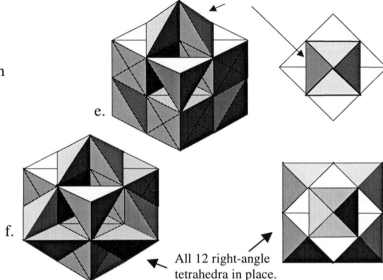

2 right-angle tetrahedra in place.

All 12 right-angle tetrahedra in place.

g. VE pattern
h. Three sets of 2 right-angle tetrahedra on 3 square faces of VE.
i. All 12 right-angle tetrahedra in a stellated form of the VE.

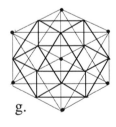 g.   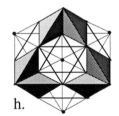 h.   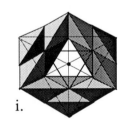 i.

This system forms an interpenetrating cube and octahedron. It is a stellated vector equilibrium pattern (3FA-25).

Two symmetrical views of the same cube/octahedron formation, from the end point of the cube and from the end point of the octahedron.

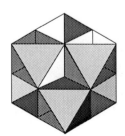 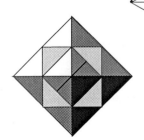

Transforming Cube

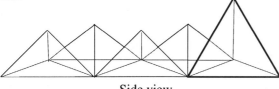
Side view

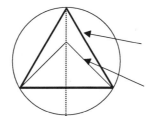

The dark line triangle represents the regular tetrahedra.

The light line triangles represent the right-angle tetrahedra.

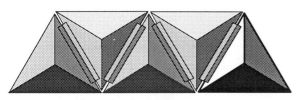
Top view

Arrange 4 right-angle tetrahedra in a line, shown on the left (3FA-90). Hinge tape each joint, attaching the long sides of the units. Hinge join a regular tetrahedron to one end (p. 28).

This hinged arrangement of tetrahedra can transform into a number of configurations. When right-angle corners are to the outside it is a cube; reversed with right-angle corners to the center it forms an octahedron with the regular tetrahedron.

Using 2-frequency tetrahedra to make cube, the space arrangement becomes more complex as it is transformed into various configurations.

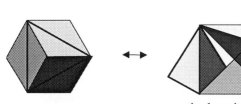
single unit system

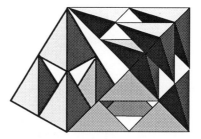
2-frequency unit system.

Transforming cube puzzle

It is instructive to make 2 hinged cubes exactly the same. Make 2 more regular tetrahedra. Do not attach them, leave them separate. Two transforming cubes and 2 regular tetrahedra combine to make a solid 2-frequency tetrahedron. This is a good spatial problem solver.

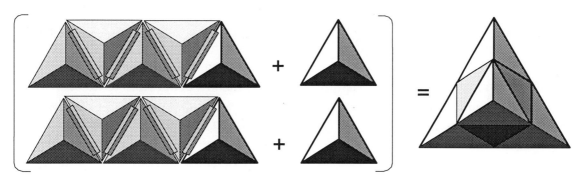

Irregular right-angle octahedron

a. Fold the equilateral triangle (3FA-5).
b. Fold each corner triangle in half, all in the same direction. This will make an irregular right-angle hexagon.
c. Fold each right-angle triangle corner half-way towards the center.
d. Join 2 circles folded this way with right-angle triangles fitting into the intervals of the other. Tape edges.

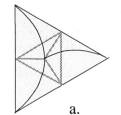
a.

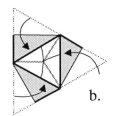
b.

tape edges together

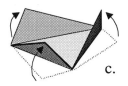
c.

plus one →

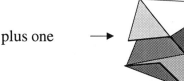
d.

→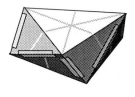

Combined 4 irregular right-angle octahedra in a tetrahedron pattern.

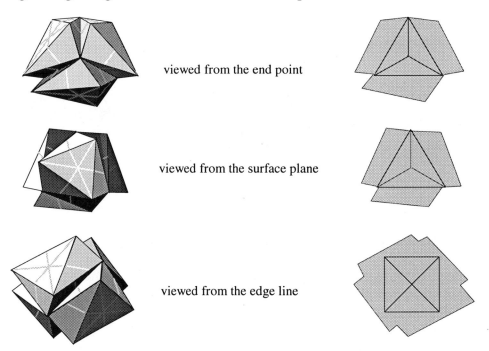

viewed from the end point

viewed from the surface plane

viewed from the edge line

    It is always useful to combine forms to themselves in the Platonic patterns, in the planer, linear, and spherical modes. It takes very little time when the class has all folded the same units and there is a lot of material to work with. It is simply a matter of finding congruent shapes and intervals that provide the means for connection. Often complexities will occur that could not have been anticipated, and sometimes it offers no further direction for development. This is a good way to watch our own consistency of process and expand our ability to search out design elements that are often unseen.

Square tube

Within the 8-frequency diameter circle lies a number of tubes. To form the square tube, the entire triangular grid need not be formed, only one diameter divided into 8 equal sections.

 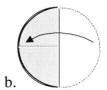 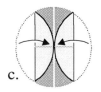 

a.   b.   c.   d.

a. Fold diameter.
b. Fold diameter in half.
c. Fold both ends of diameter to the center point and crease.
d. The diameter is divided into 4 equal parts.

  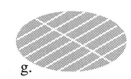 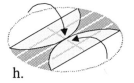

e.   f.   g.   h.

e. Fold both ends of the diameter to point of intersection on the first line on the left.
f. Fold the same on the first line on the right.
g. Open, the diameter is divided into 8 equal sections.
h. Fold both ends of the diameter to the center point.

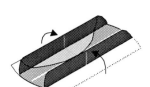 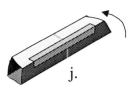

i. Fold up two outside 1/4 sections.
j. Fold edges together on middle line forming a square tube.

end view

Triangular tube

To form the triangular tube, start with folding the square tube, leaving it incomplete with 2 sides up before it goes into the square. Fold one edge into the corner of the opposite bottom fold. The fourth side is folded down over the third side to make the triangular tube. Tape the tube closed along the edge. Notice the difference in the stability and strength of the triangle tube to the square tube.

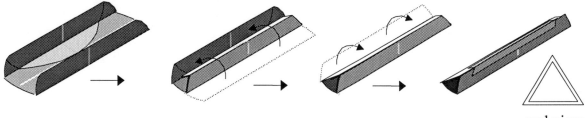

end view

Tetrahelix tube

a. Start with the full 8-frequency diameter grid.

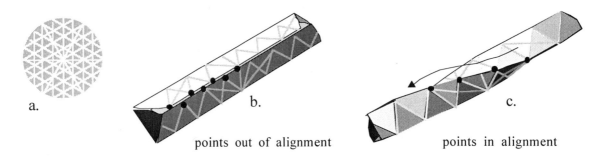

a.

b. points out of alignment

c. points in alignment

b. Fold the triangular tube. Do not tape it. Where the 2 sections of the triangular tube overlap and the corner edges meet, the crease lines do not match up (except for the center diameter line). The triangle points alternate from one side to the other.

c. Twist one side over the other until the points match up so they all meet at the edge. The diameter line no longer meets itself. This twisting motion forms a helix of triangles that define a pattern of tetrahedra face to face. Tape the edges together in this matching position (3FA-19). The helix can be right-handed or left-handed, depending on which direction the twist is made.

Octahelix tube

a. Start with the 8-frequency grid.
b. Twist the folded triangular tube into the tetrahelix, leaving it untaped.
c. Continue to twist the edge further in the same direction until the points line up with the next points on the edge. This further twisting will change the tetrahedra into octahedra joined face to face in a line. The octahelix has both right-hand and left-hand twisting, depending on the direction of spiral edge followed. This is a very different helix pattern than the one revealed in the octahedron within the tetrahelix. (3FA-22)

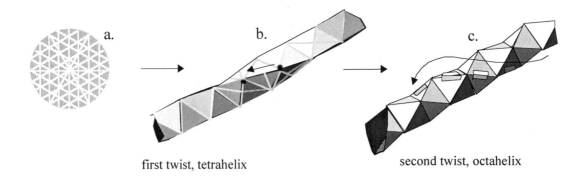

a. b. first twist, tetrahelix c. second twist, octahelix

Linear movement system

a. Folding the hexagon circle.
b. Use one of the diameters and fold it into 8 equal divisions (3FA-78).
c. Fold opposite sides of the hexagon making parallel lines to the divided diameter.
d. Next fold the ends of the diameter to the center using the creases already in the circle.
e. Fold each long edge to the centerline, recreasing the lines already there.

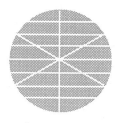
a.
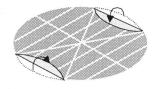
b.
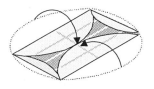
c.
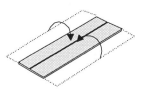
d.

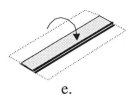
e.
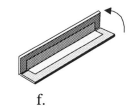
f.

e. Fold in half, one side onto the other and crease well.
f. Open until the 2 sides are perpendicular to each other. Tape the 2 edges together along the inside middle line keeping the 90° angle. This makes a right-angle channel, or "L" bar.

g. Use the hinge joint to join "L" bars end to end.

g.

h.

i.
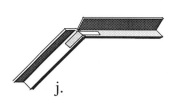
j.

h. Place together the long sides of 2 "L"s taping across the leg of the "T" end.
i. Fold the 2 "L"s in the open direction until they can't go any further. They will be in a straight line, end to end. Tape across the joint on the backside of tape.
j. Taping this way gives the greatest movement and strength to the joint.

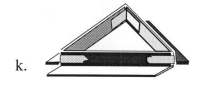
k.
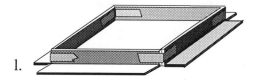
l.

k. Add one more "L" bar to make a triangle, taping with the right-angle side out.
l. Put four "L" bars into a square and tape them in the same way. Compare the movement of the square and triangle.

m. Add another "L" diagonally to the square. Move the square until it becomes stable. How does that change the square?

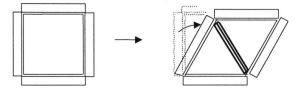

n. Using 5 "L"s make a pentagon and add 2 flat diagonals to make it stable. How does that reform the pentagon?

n. Make a hexagon and add 3 flat diagonals, moving it until it becomes stable. How has it changed?

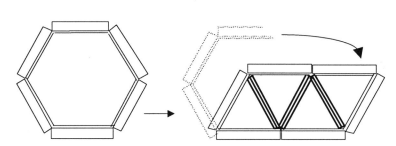

p. Using 6 individual "L" units, tape them in a tetrahedron with perpendiculars out.

q. Using 12 individual "L" units, join them to form a cube. Tape the joints on both sides making hinged connections.

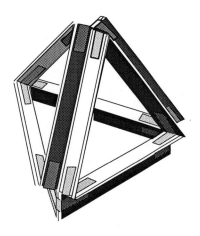
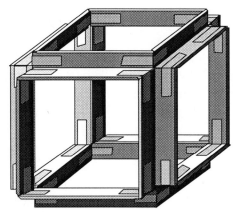

Explore the difference of the 2 forms. Use more flatten "L" bars to find positions of stability as the cube moves. How does this change the form? Will combining "L" bars work to form other polyhedra?

Hexagon 3, 4, 5

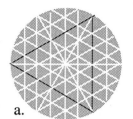 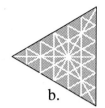 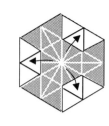

a. b. c. d.

a. Fold the 8-frequency grid circle.
b. Reform it into the large triangle.
c. Fold each point to the center and recrease the lines. This makes a hexagon shape.
d. Fold back from the center the corner point to the center of the first fold on the hexagon edge.
e. Make another the same. Join and tape them together on the unfolded hexagon edges. Also tape the folded edges where they come together. Change the angles of the folded corners to form a triangle, a square and a pentagon interval.

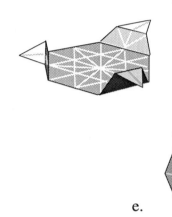 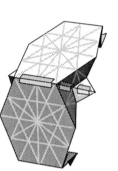

e.

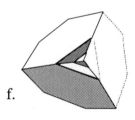 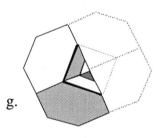 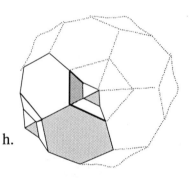

f. g. h.

f. The <u>triangle</u> pattern. Join 4 hexagons into a tetrahedron pattern. This will form a truncated tetrahedron with 4 hexagon and 4 triangle faces (p.3 4) (3FA-79). There are in-out variations to the triangle intervals.

g. The <u>square</u> pattern. Join 8 hexagon units in an octahedron pattern. This will form a truncated octahedron, with 8 hexagons and 6 square faces (p. 34, 35). Again, there are in-out variation to folding the square face.

h. The <u>pentagon</u> pattern. Join 20 hexagon units in a 5 pattern. It will form a truncated icosahedron (p. 34). There are 20 hexagons and 12 pentagon faces. Options are again there for variations with the pentagon faces.

163

3FA 106 Dodecahedron/icosahedron

a. Fold an 8-frequency diameter grid.
b. Fold it into a pentagon cone by folding in 1/6 of circle to the back.
c. Tape the flap to the inside to keep it out of the way.
d. Locate the folds showing the center pentastar and the decagon that surrounds it.
e. Folding up the curves outside the center decagon will straighten the sides and form a 2-frequency pentagon pyramid in the center.
f. Fold back circle around outside forming another pentagon outside of the center pyramid.
g. Push in the center decagon to form a center pentagon. Turn it over. The back is the reverse in-out design. Explore both sides developing larger systems. This in-out zigzag folding is a simple reflection of the first fold of the circle, amplified by folding the 3 diameters and compounded by frequency development.

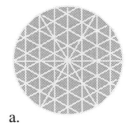
a.

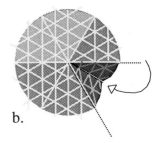
b.

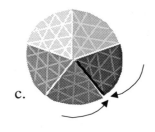
c.

d.

e.

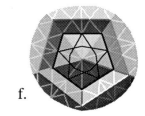
f.

h. Go back to step (f) without center pushed in, locate the 5 points of intersection of the pentagon star.
i. Push down on these 5 points and the star will pop out.
j. Make 12 units and put them together edge to edge, curved flaps to the inside, in a dodecahedron pattern. Notice the star points form an icosahedron pattern.

g.

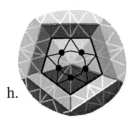
h.

i.

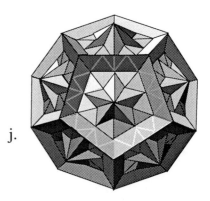
j.

164

3-frequency pentagon variations

a. Fold an 8-frequency circle.
b. Find the largest hexagon on the bisecting diameters.
c. Fold curved edges over on the hexagon lines.
d. Fold one corner to the center point.
e. Fold them individually all to the center point.
f. Turn over. Bisecting diameters are now the star points.
g. Push in line between star points.
h. It forms a pentacap pyramid.
i. Locate the small pentagon in the middle and push it in making a pentagonal depression.
j. Locate the lines that form a star and the line between the points.
k. Fold in on those lines making the star.
l. Change the creased edge from the star points to center star to the crease that defines another pentagon connecting the points of star intersections.
m. Push star points to the back bringing points together. Half-opening the star points and joining to another will form an icosahedron pattern (3AF-44).
n. Push mid-points of outside edges in so that each star point becomes the end point of a small octahedra.
o. Make a change in line emphasis by pushing in on the mid-line of each edge of the pentagon depression. Push in between the star points as you form the creases that run from the center point out to the star points.

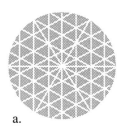
a.
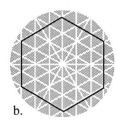
b.
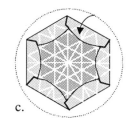
c.

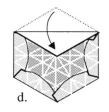
d.
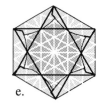
e.
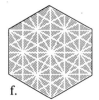
f.

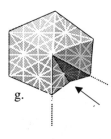
g.
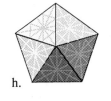
h.

i.

j.
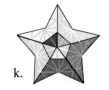
k.

l.

m

n.

o.

The variations of these folds can be used as multiple units for any number of designs. The scale is different than other pentagon forms because this comes from a 3-frequency folding rather than an even number division. Try combining different scales in 3, 4 and 5 pattern folding as you explore systems.

Bisection development of 8-frequency grid

a. Fold an 8-frequency grid. Then fold the 6 lines that form the hexagon on the circumference, connecting the star points. This divides the sides of the hexagon into a 4-frequency pattern.

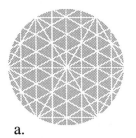
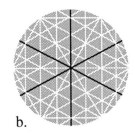
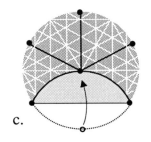
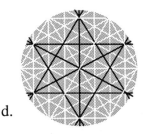

a. b. c. d.

b. Trace the 3 bisecting diameters already folded.
c. Fold one of the end points onto the center point and crease.
d. Fold the remaining end points of the 3 diameters to the center point forming a star. The end points do not meet on the circumference, rather on the mid-points of the sides of the outermost hexagon.

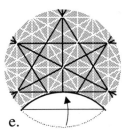
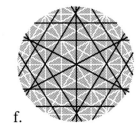

e. f.

e. Fold the endpoint of a diameter to the first new point of intersection on that diameter just folded.
f. Do that to the other 5 diameter points. Observe the new folded lines and how they start bisecting the small triangles.
g. Notice how many different sizes of triangular grids there are in this folded matrix, and the different proportional systems.

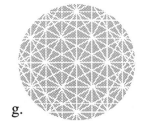

g.

h. By continuing the same process of folding the edge points of the bisecting diameters to the newly generated points of intersection, the 8-frequency will reach another scale or coherent pattern division. Each small triangle is now bisected in 3 directions forming even smaller triangles.

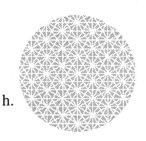

h.

166

Folding Pi

"Pi" represents a number describing the difference between the diameter of a circle and the circumference, the measure, and the boundary. The straight line and circle can never be resolved equally, they are different. The circle is principle, it is whole. The diameter is the first division of the circle, always a part expression of movement within the wholeness of the circle. Curved line segments are the visible aspect of the unseen whole circle. The constructed images are partial reflections of what is without containment.

1. Start with the large folded equilateral triangle. Fold it on the 3 bisecting diameters into the hexagon shape (3FA-6). There are 3 sets of 2 radial length chords each, touching around the circumference. The hexagon is a straight line expression of the measure of the circle and the difference is irreconcilable. The area between the hexagon and the circumference is the difference between the hexagon as a part and the circle as whole.

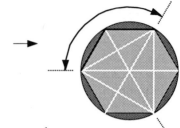

2. a. Fold the circle back into the large triangle and with a pencil or pen, trace around the curved edges. Put in turn each folded edge on top and trace completely.
   b. When you open the circle flat and turn it over, you will find that tracing the curves has formed small vesicas around each in-side of the hexagon.
   c. The area of 3 vesicas plus the area of the hexagon itself will equal the area of the circle.

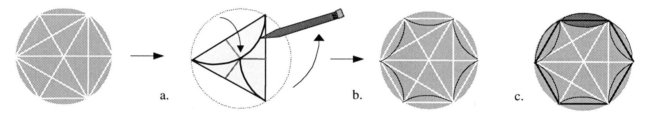

The width of one vesica plus 3 diameter lengths is very close to the length of the circumference, but not quite equal, for they are straight lines and never complete.

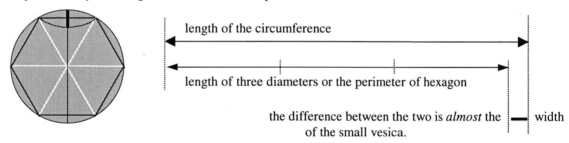

The length of diameters and circumference will change with the size of the circle. The proportional difference between them does not change with size, it is <u>constant</u>. Because the straight line will never equal the circle, the number that represents that difference is: **.14159265358214808651**...without end.

Usually only the first 4 numbers are used, **.1415**. Then adding the **3** diameters, the number becomes 3.1415..... This number is constant to all sizes of circles. This number is called **Pi**. The symbol used to represent 3.1415 is π.

The length of the circumference (**C**) equals the diameter (**D**) times the constant 3.1415, or C = D x 3.1415 or C=Dπ or C = 2rπ (the diameter divided in half is 2 radii). To prove the number constant, divide both sides by the diameter for any size circle;

$$\frac{C}{D} = \frac{D\pi}{D} \quad \text{or} \quad \frac{C}{D} = \pi$$

The measure goes into the whole 3 times plus a difference of endless expression.

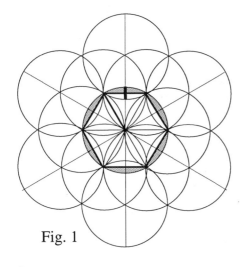

Fig. 1

The matrix of 13 circles generates a proportional relationship observed in all circles (fig 1). The radial bisector to the edge length of the hexagon reduces that length on the circumference by one-half, making 12 equal divisions in the circle. Continued reduction by one-half of each successive length, the bisector will never coincide with the diameter, for it only goes half the distance each time. The right-angle measured division of the whole will never be whole. The divisions will make smaller straight lines with an increasing number of sides (fig 2). Each polygon successively has twice the number of sides as the one before, 6, 12, 24, 48, 96... The straight line intervals get shorter and the difference ratio proportionally decreases. The n-sided polygon is never the circle.

Keep in mind the bisector is a diameter and happens on 2 parts of the circumference, in all 6 areas of the hexagonal division.

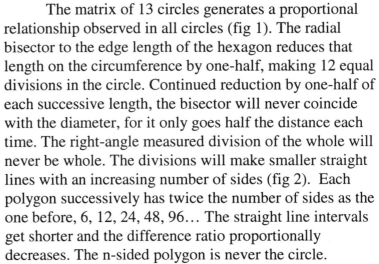

Fig. 2

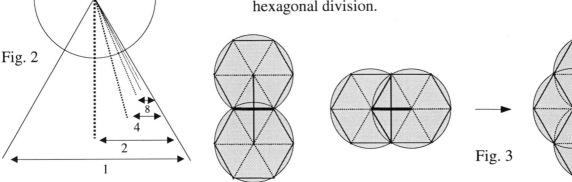

Fig. 3

There are only 2 ways 2 circles can share the same radius: vertically and horizontally. This right-angle function shows them both the same (fig 3). The small vesica is found within and perpendicular to the large vesica. The long axis of each vesica divide the other in half. The circles are all joined in the same hexagon pattern of intersection and division that forms the matrix reflection of the hexagon measure of the circle. This indicates a relationship between the right-angle division and Pi. This happens in 3 orientations.

The symbol for Pi, when viewed in context of the circle matrix is formed to the difference between the diameter and circumference. It shows the proportional function of the 2 radii with the difference between them being the width of the small vesica. It shows Pi to be an endless wave function between the circle whole and the straight line parts (fig 4).

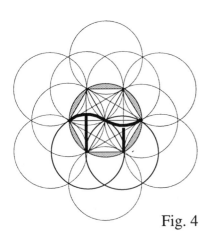

Fig. 4

It may be coincidental, but it is interesting to note there is no difference between symbol and function, particularly when the nature of the circle demonstrates implicate order. Form and function is an abstracted concept of separation that has no reality.

Pythagorean Theorem

1. Mark any 2 points, A and B on the circumference of a circle.
2. Fold points A and B exactly together.
3. A diameter is formed with 2 end points called C and D.
4. Form a line connecting points A and B by folding the diameter CD onto itself showing line AB at a right-angle to the CD, intersecting at point E.
5. Trace a line around the folded circumference with a pencil and mark the intersection F where traced line crosses the diameter CD.
6. The traced line AFB and the curved edge ACB form a <u>vesica</u> where the vertical and horizontal lines divided each other in half at point E, forming 4 right-triangles. The 4 hypotenuse of these 4 right-angles are congruent, AC=BC=BF=AF.
7. This division shows 2 right-hand right-triangles, AEF and CEB, and 2 left-hand triangles, AEC and BEF. We can then say that AE to itself EB plus EF to itself CE will produce AF to itself CB. Rephrasing this, AE squared + EF squared = AF squared. Giving it more general terms by making AE =A and EF=B and AE =C, we can say:

$$A^2 + B^2 = C^2$$

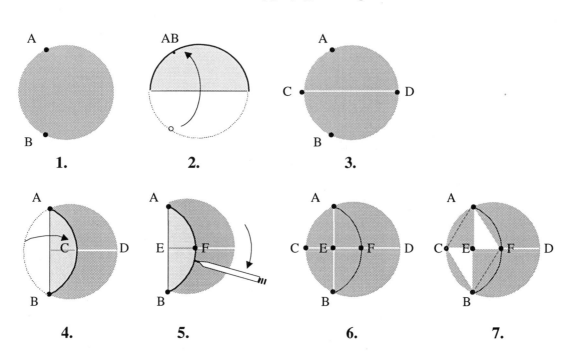

169

Pythagorean Theorem continues

In folding the circle, the Pythagorean Theorem first appears as a function of the vesica intersection of the circle to itself. It is no different in drawing 2 intersecting circles. It all takes place within the vesica intersection. This is not standard proof for the Pythagorean Theorem. It is logically consistent with proportional movement of the circle to itself. It is an effect of the self-referenced movement of the whole in the form of a circle.

This observation offers no conflict to traditional proof, which developed abstractly using only a right-angle triangle. The truth of this generalization is not self-evident in the isolated single right-triangle. The meaningfulness of the proof is in the context. Geometry has provided an effective showcase for a system of logical thinking that results in the abstract "proof" of any given statement based on the "provability" of previous statements. This way of thinking has become the bases for mathematics, the sciences and the evolution of technological development, and a generally accepted way of processing information, but it is not about geometry, nor is it comprehensive.

By observing the right-angle triangle in the greatest context the logic and truth of why it is so important in the development of mathematics becomes clear; it happens first. When presented in the abstract, one does not know where formulas and theorems have come from or exactly what they represent, or why they work. We do not know what has been left out for the sake of simplicity, which limits our ability to make meaningful connections.

This theorem describes the function of the vesica, the rhomboid shared by each circle as an expression of a single radius. The self-reflecting circle generates proportional right-angle movement as seen in the first movement of the circle. Right-angle expression of movement is the very nature of folding the circle. The Pythagorean Theorem reflects the whole circle moved to the power of itself or the circle times itself, self-generation. This generalization must hold true for all subsequent right-angle functions, regardless of size or proportion. It is principled to duality inherently expressed by two right-hand and two left-hand, right-angle triangles. Seeing the right-angle function in the context of the circle extends its meaning beyond formulation.

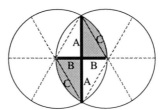 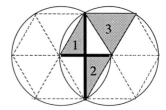

A to itself, added to B to itself reveals C to itself

or

A squared plus B squared equals C squared

or

$$A^2 + B^2 = C^2$$

Area 1 + area 2 = area 3

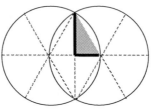 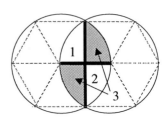

<u>Fermat's theorem</u> is $X^n + Y^n = Z^n$

      This is a generalization about the right-angle function. The letters stand for any quantity, and the (n) as any number larger than 2. Nobody has been able to prove that it works where (n) is a number larger than 2. One person is said to have worked out the proof, but it is so long and complex that nobody else has been able to verify it. Possibly it is about primary proportional duality of movement and not about the infinitude of numbers. Maybe that is why Fermat's numbers beyond two may never work.

      Higher number forms may not embody the quality and simplicity of the first singular right-angle movement. It is quit possible that mathematics is in evolutionary partnership with cosmic development and that the potential of universal forming is in process. Or maybe we are on an evolving tangent of separation. This is a good problem for older students to think about. It is as much a philosophical question as it is a mathematical one with very real implications towards how we think about each other and our relationship to the universe. It is about the ordering and evolutionary formation of parts within the whole.

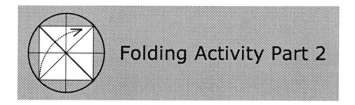

Folding the circle into a 4-8 Pattern

Folding the 4-8 proportions is the same process as folding the 3-6 diameters. The difference is in the proportions of the 1:2 ratio that generates 4 diameters rather than 3. The diameters are the same. It is the circumference intervals between them that create different angulation. The principles are constant having been generated in the first fold of the circle and primary to all three proportional folding. Working with the 4-8 symmetry is about a differently proportioned triangular grid, but triangular none the less.

As the diameters are developed to a higher frequency grid the more potential it will generate. While the square grid pattern is probably most familiar, we shall see that it is limited in regards to the hexagon, as also is the pentagon limited (p. 42). The full potential of both is always within the triangle/hexagon pattern of order. None in this process of formation is separate from each other: it all forms triangulation within the singularity of the circle form.

Folding the square pattern

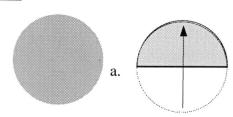 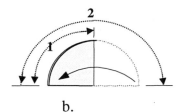 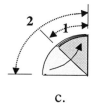 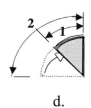

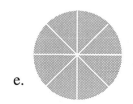

a. Fold the circle in half, a ratio of 1:2.
b. Take one end point and fold it around to the opposite point.
c. Take one of the 2 folded corner points and fold it back over to the opposite corner point.
d. Take the remaining corner point and fold that behind to the opposite corner. Crease well when all edges are even.
e. Open circle and observe the 4 diameters.

Having folded 4 diameters, reconfigure them exploring different forms that can be made; the same process as with 3 diameters (3FA-2). The most important configuration is reducing the octagon down to a hexagon patterned cone that will reform into the right-angle tetrahedron.

Spherical octahedron

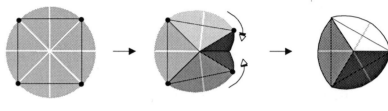

Bring 2 end points of a square pattern together folding center crease to the inside. Fold over, tape to the inside face forming a right-angle tetrahedron pattern.

a.

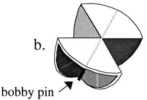
b.
bobby pin

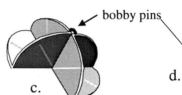
bobby pins
c.

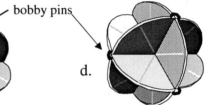
d.

a. Fold 4 circles the same.
b. Join together on the straight edges; use bobby pin to hold them together.
c. Do the same with the other 2 folded circles. Adjust them both to make right-angle tetrahedron intervals the same size as the right-angle formed tetrahedra.
d. Put the 2 sets together so they generate 4 more right-angle tetrahedral intervals, hold them with bobby pins. This will form the spherical octahedron pattern showing 3 great circles.

Notice 4 folded circles were joined and only 3 are evident. One quarter of each has been folded in, giving the appearance of eliminating one complete circle. The 4 only work in the context of triangulation.

This form of spherical pattern of the octahedron can be seen where the center of the triangular planes push in meeting at the center. If the same center point were pushed out to the same distance it would become an octahedral star or cube pattern where by connecting the end points would form the 6 square faces of the cube. This is the number of points of the octahedron. Again it is important to understand that individual shapes have little meaning without the context of pattern in which they have been generated.

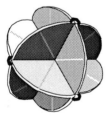
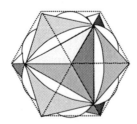
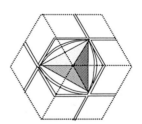

Spherical octahedron variation

Fold a circle into the 4-8 pattern. Fold in 4 flaps making straight edges between the 4 points that form one of the squares in the circle. The other 2 diameters become bisecting diameters. Now fold in 1/4 of the circle making a right-angle tetrahedron. The curved edges can be folded in or out or flat to the triangular plane. They can be used to join to other forms.

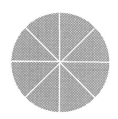 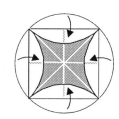  

Triangle/square transformation

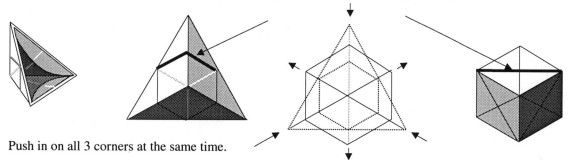

The hexagon and triangle are reciprocal by in-out movement

Push in on all 3 corners at the same time.

The corners of the tetrahedron when pushed towards the center will reform into half of a cube. Two half-cubes when joined together edge to edge, each square fitting into square intervals of the other, form a cube. Two right-angled tetrahedron will make one cube.

4-frequency diameter circle

   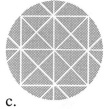 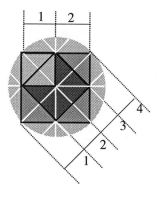

a.   b.   c.

a. Fold curved edges over to form the square shape.
b. Fold each corner point to center point and crease well.
c. Open circle flat and look at the pattern of folded lines.
   The square is 2-frequency and the diameter is 4-frequency.

Small cube

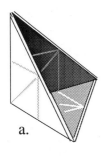

a. Fold a 4-frequency diameter circle into a right-angle tetrahedron.
b. Fold each of the 3 corner points inside on the mid-line creases that form smaller 3-square half-cube.
c. Put 2 of these together to make a cube.

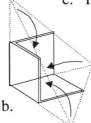

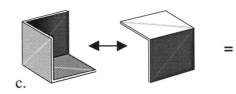

a.

b.

c.

Variation on small cube

a. Fold in 2 corners of the tetrahedron instead of all 3.
b. Make another the same and join them in opposites forming a cube.
Make more of these units and explore different ways they go together.

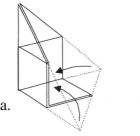

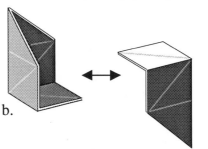

a.

b.

Right-angle octahedron

a. Start with folding above (4FA-7).
b. Push down square on diagonal crease.
c. Push out on side points. Put open interval on flat surface so all 4 points are on a single plane.
d. Make 2 the same way, join and tape on the open edges for an octahedron of right-angle triangles.

a.

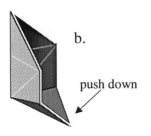

b.

push down

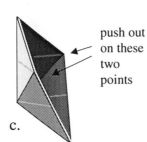

push out on these two points

c.

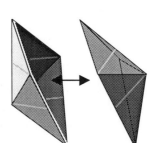

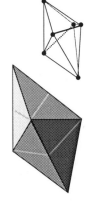

d.

Inside out stellated cube

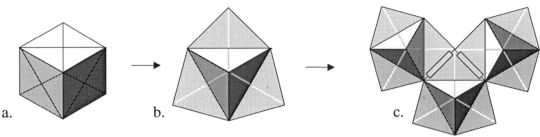

a.   b.   c.

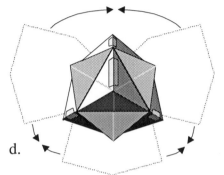

d.

a. Start by folding the half cube, 3 squares (4FA-4).
b. Fold triangular half of squares out to form a flat plane leaving the right-angle tetrahedron standing in the center of a right-angle hexagon.
c. Fold 2 more the same and tape all 3 hexagons around a common center, forming 3 sides of a square.
d. Fold the square into a tetrahedron by bringing the two edges together and taping. Bring the 3 sets of open edges together at all 3 corners of a center tetrahedron and tape closed.

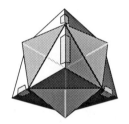 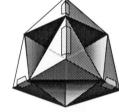

Tetrahedra pointing out   Tetrahedra pointing to center

Octahedron cube combinations

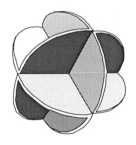 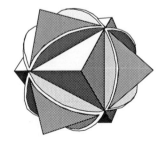 

Join right-angle tetrahedra, cubes, and the spherical octahedron exploring various combinations that can be generated from the congruency of shapes, and movement of scaling.

4-Frequency again

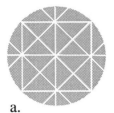 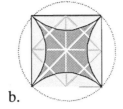 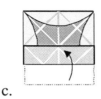 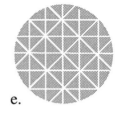

a.   b.   c.   d.   e.

a. Fold a 4-frequency square grid.
b. Fold curved sides over forming the square.
c. Fold one edge to the center line parallel to the edge.
d. Open fold and do that to the other 3 sides forming a square. The corners of the new square will correspond to the mid-points of the larger square.
e. Notice the circle is still a 4-frequency pattern, yet there is another level of smaller right-triangles.

 Curved triangle

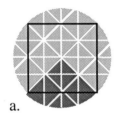 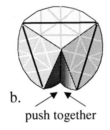 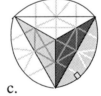 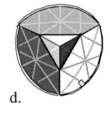

a.   b.   c.   d.

push together

a. Locate a quarter of the large square.
b. Fold in quarter on center line.
c. Tape flap to inside surface.
d. Fold circle up around small tetrahedron formed in the middle.
e. Turn over and fold curves over on large triangle.
f. Join 2 units together on the curved flaps using bobby pins in corners.
g. Put 2 sets of 2 units together joining in the same way as the first set. This forms a tetrahedron pattern.
h. Join 4 sets of 2 each into a square pattern.

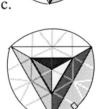 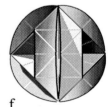

e.   f.

g.

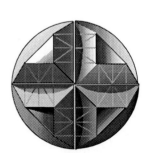

h.

i. Make 2 sets of 4 folded triangles.
j. Put the 2 sets together in the same way as before.
   This forms an octahedron pattern.

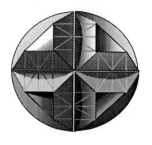

 Fractal development

a. Make the octahedral unit shown in (3FA-67). Start with the 8-frequency grid so tetrahedral depression can be folded into center.

b. Make 4 units, for alternate triangular faces of the above octahedron sphere (4FA-12). This forms a tetrahedron pattern.

c. Make 4 more and attach them to remaining 4 faces. This completes the octahedron pattern. Both units are the same pattern, formed similarly in different scales.

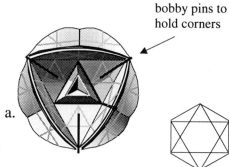

bobby pins to hold corners

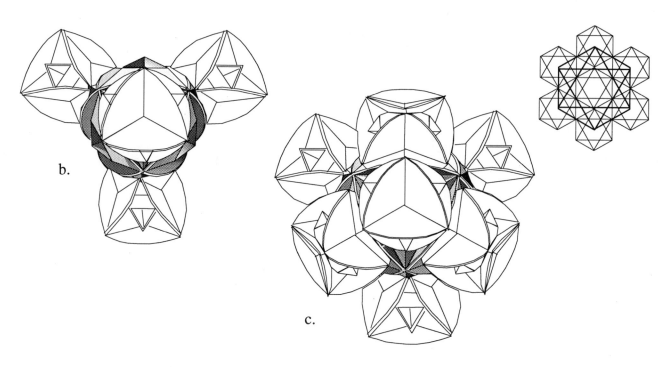

Curved triangle again

a. Make 4 circle triangular units (4FA-12e).

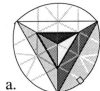
a.

b. Tape 2 of them together joining the curved flaps so that the creases are parallel with the center tetrahedra pointing to the outside. Tape on both sides of flaps.

c. Fold the 2 taped units making a tetrahedral interval of the same size as the units.

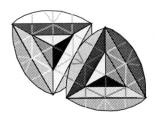
b.

c.

d. Make another set of 2 in the same way. Put the 2 sets of 2 together attaching the curved edges in parallel as before, one at right-angle to the other in a tetrahedron pattern forming a cube in the center.

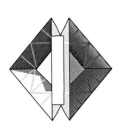
d.

view of edge line

view of end point

8-frequency diameter circle

We have seen that there are 2 levels of folding the 4-frequency square grid. One (4FA5) shows the diameters and edge lengths divided into 4 equal sections. Continuing to fold the grid the diameters remain in 4 divisions and the edge lengths of the inscribed square increases to 4 divisions. This is complete expression of the 4-frequency diameter grid, though it is useful to work with the uncompleted grid sometimes.

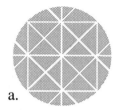 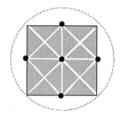 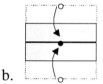

a. b.

a. Start with the folded 4-frequency diameter circle and fold into the square shape (4FA-1, 5).
b. Fold the mid-point on each edge to the center point, making 2 sets of parallel lines perpendicular to each other. It remains a 4-frequency diameter/diagonal (4FA-11).

c. d. e. f.

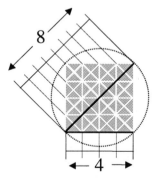

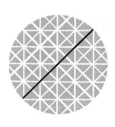

c. Locate the 4 vertex points on the 2 diagonals (diameters) that divide them each into 4 equal segments.
d. Fold the 2 end points to both points on the diagonal.
e. Repeat with the 2 end points to the points on the other diagonal.
f. The 2 diameters are now divided into 8 equal parts, becoming 8-frequency diameters to the circle.

The length of the diagonal and the edge length of the square have no common divisor. The relationship between the divisions is not one-half even though the edge is 4 and the diagonal/diameter is 8. The unit lengths are different. The diameter is the measure of the circle and the edge length is the measure of the square. One is the measure of the whole and the other a measure of one part of the whole.

Square faced vector equilibrium

This is another way to make the vector equilibrium pattern using the square to form the inverted right-angle tetrahedron interval.

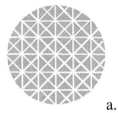 a. 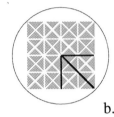 b.  c.  d.

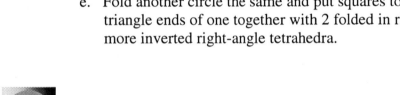 e.

a. Start with an 8-frequency grid.
b. Fold in one quarter from the corner to the center, taping flap to the inside, forming a right-angle tetrahedron.
c. Locate the center hexagon, half a cube.
d. Push in to form inverted right-angle tetrahedron making the 3 squares on each edge of the triangular interval.
e. Fold another circle the same and put squares together corner to corner bringing right-triangle ends of one together with 2 folded in right-triangles of the other making 6 more inverted right-angle tetrahedra.

3/4 cube

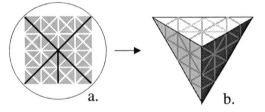 a. b. c. 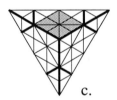 d. 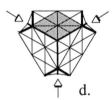 e

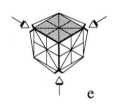 f.

a. Fold the 8-frequency circle into the square.
b. Fold in 1/4 forming a right-angle tetrahedron.
c. Locate the folds on each corner.
d. Push corners on creased edges toward the back.
e. Continue to push to the inside at back 3 squares of the 1/2 cube will form.
f. Turn over and tape flaps to the inside wall. This forms 3/4 of a cube.

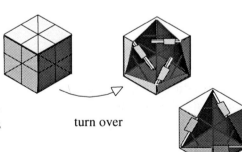

turn over

tape flaps to inside

3/4 cube, vector equilibrium

This 3/4 cube (4FA-17) has one right-angle tetrahedron corner missing from three corner points leaving an equilateral triangle opening surrounded by 3 right-angle triangles and 3 squares. All 3 shapes are basic to the VE matrix. Here we shall explore another arrangement of these same shapes and forms.

a.

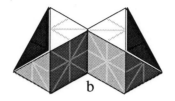

b.

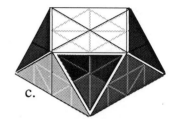

c.

a. Start with two 3/4 cubes.
b. Join together symmetrically with open triangles opposite each other, forming 2 right-angle intervals.
c. Fill the intervals with 2 more 3/4 cubes with open triangles facing out. There is a square on top and a larger square on the bottom.
d. Make another set of 4 units and put them together joining the large squares to each other. These 8 units show the 3 right-angle axes of the octahedron inside the center space.
e. When the 8 right-angle tetrahedra are placed onto the triangle openings of the VE, all 3/4 cubes are complete.

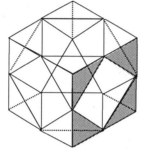

d.

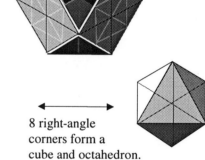

8 right-angle corners form a cube and octahedron.

e.

2-frequency 8 cubes

4-frequency 64 cubes

f.

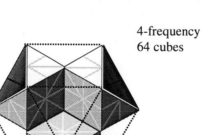

g.

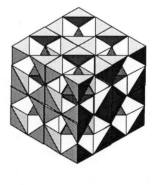

f. Use two units of b. above.
g. Join in opposite orientation (4FA-2), into a Vector Equilateral pattern.

h. The ¾ cube and the octahedron combined in an all-space filling cubic pattern of spherical order.

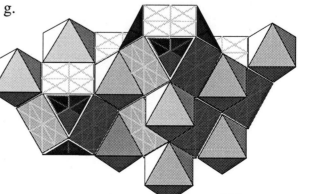

Transforming cube

a. Join two 3/4 cubes with half square sides together, open triangles to the insides.

b. Tape along edge where 2 square sides meet with a hinge joint.

c. Make another set of 2 in the same way.

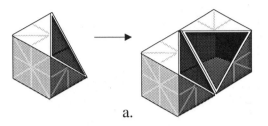
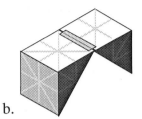
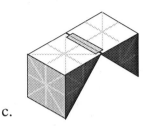

d. Put 2 sets of 2 together in an open square with the hinges on opposite sides.

e. Turn over and hinge tape one half of edge perpendicular to the line of first 2 hinges. Do not tape across center edges. Make sure you tape both sides of edge joint.

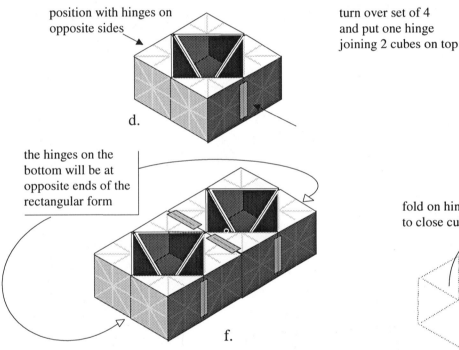
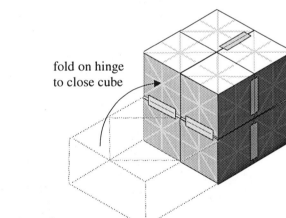

f. Put 2 sets of four 3/4 cubes taped as shown together side to side with the tape hinges on the sides parallel, and the ones on the bottom at opposite ends. Put tape hinges on the top edges holding the two halves together.

g. The cube holds 8 right-angle tetrahedra in octahedron form.

h. The movement of the 8 cubes is in the right-angle pattern of the torus (3F-21).

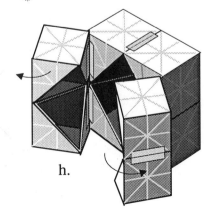

Rhombicuboctahedron

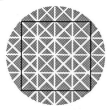 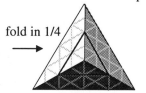 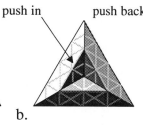 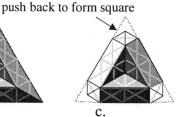

a. Fold an 8-frequency circle and fold circumference behind reforming into a square.
b. Folding in 1/4 of the square, push in on the creases of the center triangle.
c. At each corner push back on the edge line to form a flat square end.

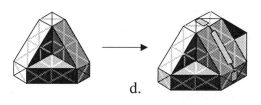 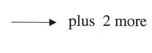 

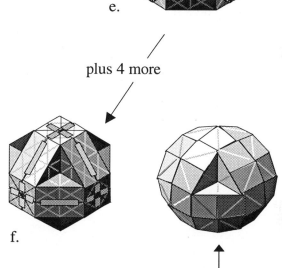

d. Tape together 2 of the same unit on the long edges and 2 square edges, making a square face.
e. Make another set of 2 the same way and tape together with an octagon open base and a square on top, now a set of 4 triangles and 4 squares.
f. Make another set of 4 and tape together the edges of the octagon. This forms a truncated pattern (p. 34, 35).

Rhombicuboctahedron sphere

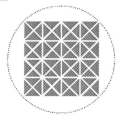 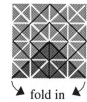 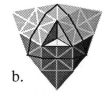 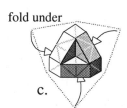 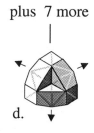

a. Fold circle into a square.
b. Fold square into a triangle with inverted center.
c. Fold the 3 corners behind and flatten square ends.
d. By pushing out a little on mid-points of each side, it will round the edges to more of a curved triangle, a more ball-like shape when all 8 units are put together.

Cuberoot tetrahedron

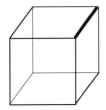 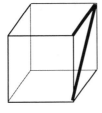 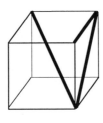 

1.   2.   3.   4.

There are 3 primary root measures to the cube.
1. The length of the side.
2. The diagonal to the square face.
3. The diagonal through the center from one corner to the opposite corner. These 3 lengths form an expanding spiral defined by 4 of the 8 points of the cube. Two opposite spiral are shown.
4. The 3 root measures of the cube define a tetrahedron of specific proportions.

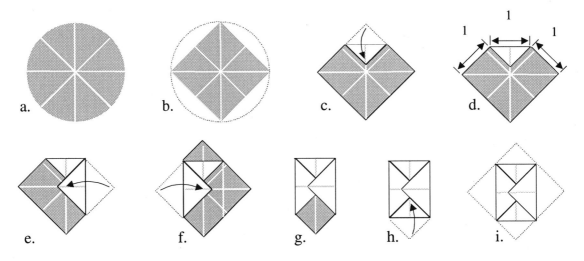

a. Start with the 4 diameter folded circle.
b. Fold it square.
c. Fold the top corner straight down the vertical diagonal line until the length of the top folded edge is equal to the resultant lengths of each side.
d. All 3 edges on top of the horizontal diameter will be equal.
e. Fold the right-hand corner across the centerline so the edge of triangle meets the edge of the triangle fold on top making a right-angle corner.
f. Open that fold and do the same thing to the opposite side on the left.
g. Refold (e) and (f), one back over the other leaving a square-shaped opening at the bottom between them.
h. Fold up bottom corner, edges meeting folded-over edges from the sides.
i. This divides the square into a proportional rectangle shape.

j. Open the square and find a diagonal line between 2 opposite corner points of the rectangle in the square.
k. Fold on that diagonal line through the center of the square. It will make an irregular half division of the square proportional to the rectangle.

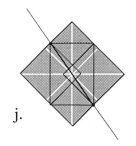
j.

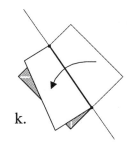
k.

bring edges together

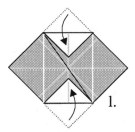
l.

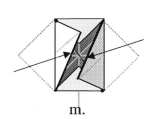
m.

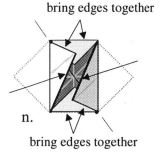
n.

bring edges together

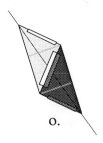
o.

l. Open the square and fold the top and bottom triangle on creased rectangle lines.
m. Fold side triangle flaps of the rectangle leaving half-open.
n. Fold on the creased diagonal of the rectangle. As you do that, bring the 2 side triangles together. Bring the top edge of one triangle to the top edge of the rectangle. At the same time bring the bottom edge of other triangle to bottom edge of the rectangle.
o. All the right-angles fit together. A tetrahedron is formed that is all right-angle isosceles triangles, 2 each of 2 different sizes.
p. One cuberoot tetrahedron is 1/6 of a cube. It shows one-half of 2 faces of the cube. There is a right-hand and left-hand rootcube tetrahedron.

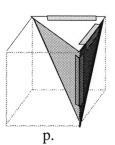
p.

q. Right and left-handedness is determined by the direction of the diagonal to the folded rectangle. Fold to the left and it is a left-handed tetrahedron.
r. Fold the diagonal to the right for a right-hand tetrahedron.
s. It will take 3 right-hand and 3 left-hand cuberoot tetrahedra to make a complete cube.

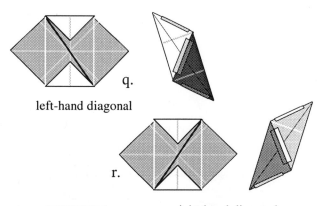
q.
left-hand diagonal

r.
right-hand diagonal

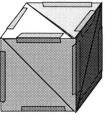
s.

Cuberoot cube

It will take 3 right-hand and 3 left-hand cuberoot tetrahedra to make a complete cube. This is another way to see the hexagon, 6 triangles, as it is revealed by an inherent division of the cube pattern.

a. Hinge join 6 cuberoot tetrahedra together in the pattern of the tetrahelix (3FA-19).

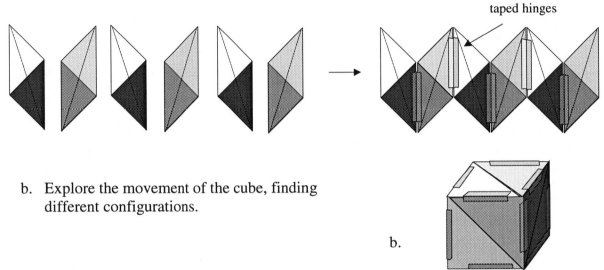

b. Explore the movement of the cube, finding different configurations.

Double cube torus

Eight is the minimum number of tetrahedra that will form into a tours (3FA-21). To put the cuberoot tetrahedra into a torus will take 12, two full cubes. It will take 6 right-hand tetrahedra and 6 left-hand tetrahedra hinged taped together into a ring. The torus becomes more complex with 18 units, 3 cubes.

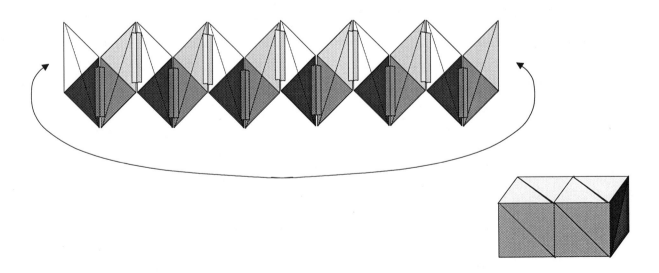

Cube octahedron

   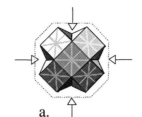

a. b.

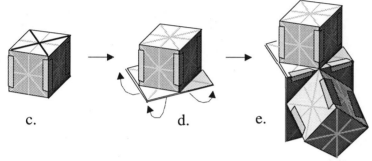

c. d. e.

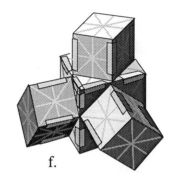

f.

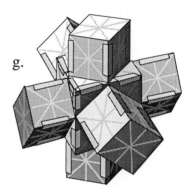

a. Start by folding the octagon cross.
b. Continue to fold the squares together forming a cube. Tape edges together.
c. The bottom triangular flaps will close the cube.
d. In this case fold the bottom flaps out so they form a flat square on the same plane as the square opening.
e. Make another cube the same way and join the flat bottom squares together on the edges.
f. Make a third cube the same and tape the flat square bottom to the other 2 flat squares forming the corner of half of a larger cube.
g. Make another unit of 3 the same way and join them together forming a complete larger cube with 6 cubes off of each side.
The 6 cubes form an octahedron pattern that define the VE square and triangle pattern seen on the faces of the large center cube.

g.

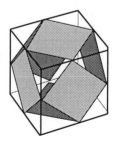

189

Transformational octagon cross

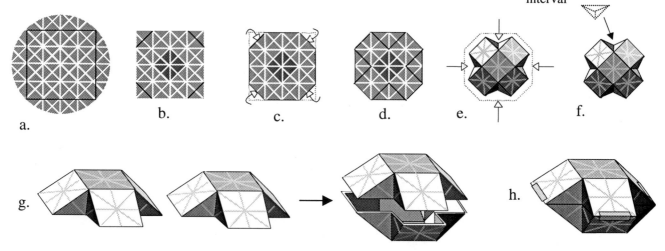

a. Fold the 8-frequency diameter circle.
b. Fold it into the square shape and locate the corner triangles.
c. Fold each corner triangle under and crease well. Locate the 2-frequency center square.
d. This square forms a cross with 4 of the same size squares on each side.
e. Push in on center crease of triangles between the 4 squares.
f. This makes a shape of 5 square faces and 4 right-angle tetrahedra intervals.
g. Make 2 the same and put the open cross edges together.
h. Tape them <u>only</u> where the square edges come together on the 4 sides.

Below are a few of many transformational relationships to be explored within this system. The 4 untaped tetrahedral intervals are important for the movement. It also makes it easy to get a finger inside to pop creases out when necessary.

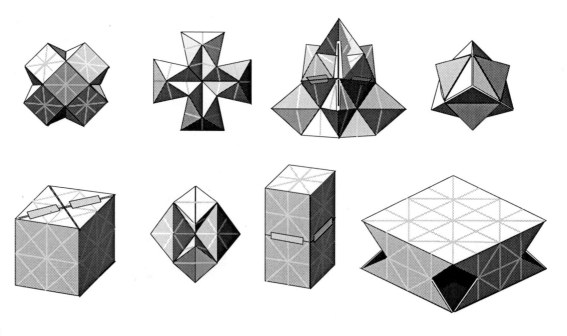

Variation in a cube

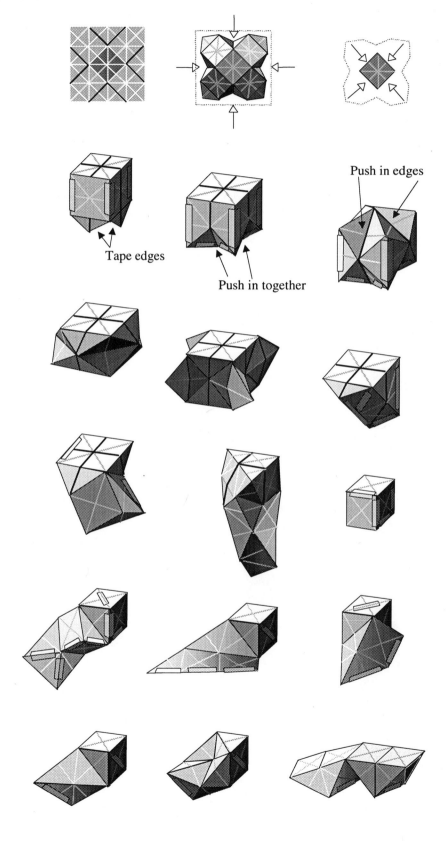

Fold an 8-frequency square grid into the circle. Configure into a cube (4FA-23c). Begin to push in and out on the folded lines finding edges and shapes that are congruent. Look for symmetrical relationships and develop those directions. Try to identify specific personalities of different forms and arrangements of the right-angle triangles. That is often a clue to knowing how to develop it into more complex systems.

Combine multiple units to themselves. Combine units to each other. Combine them with other foldings that have congruent and proportional relationships. Explore the potential of this part of the circle.

191

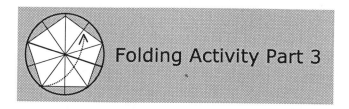

Folding the circle into a 5-10 Pattern

Folding the 5-10 proportional grid follows the same principles and process as folding the 3-6 and 4-8, yet it forms a very different proportional system (p. 43). There is a specific growth ratio of progression where each level of growth is predicated on the proportional division that precedes it. The 5 fold symmetry is called the "golden ratio," or "golden mean." This ratio is consistant back to the single measure of origin as it evolves endless levels of complex growth. It is evident through out nature, though most identifiable in pentagon forms. It is usually illustrated in the growth ratio of the Chambred Nautilus shell and the arrangement of seeds in the sunflower. There are many sources available for information about the golden ratio proportion.

In the pentagon, the edge length is proportional to the diagonals that form the pentagon star. This is the same edge-to-diagonal relationship of the 3-6 and 4-8, with different proportions. They all function in the same way, showing different ratios. It all goes back to circumference to diameter/diagonal relationship in the first fold of the undivided circle, which is a reflection of relationships of the formed and unformed inherent to spherical order.

Folding the pentagon pattern

 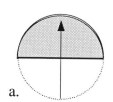 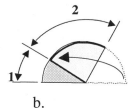 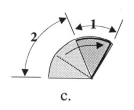 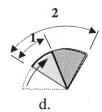

a.   b.   c.   d.

a. Fold the circle in half.
b. Fold the right-hand corner around the circumference until it looks like the part just folded is twice the amount of the part left.
c. Fold the part just folded, in half, folding the left corner back around to the right-hand corner.
d. Fold the remainder on the left in half bringing the left-hand corner to the edge of the previous fold. The 2 folded parts should be equal.
e. Fold this in half; bring one corner behind to the other corner. When all corners and edges are even, give a good strong crease.
f. Open up the circle and find 5 diameters, 10 equal divisions. The circle has been folded 5 times to a ratio of 1:2.

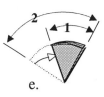

e.

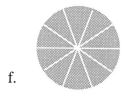

f.

193

Icosadodecahedron sphere

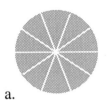 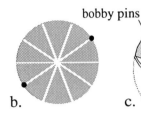 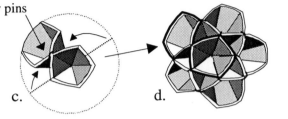 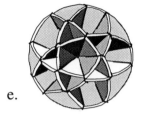

a. b. c. d. e.

a. Fold 5 diameters into the circle.
b. Bring together both end of one diameter.
c. Hold the 2 ends together with a bobby pin. There will be 5 sections on each side. Two 5-sided pyramids joined by common edge.
d. Make 2 more units in the same way and join all 3 sets touching only on the edges forming tetrahedron spaces between then. Use bobby pins to hold them together.
e. Make another set of 3 the same way. Join them both together forming more tetrahedra making a sphere. It is an icosadodecahedron pattern, one of the 13 semi-regular polyhedron (p. 34, 35). It combines 20 triangles of the icosahedron and 12 pentagons of the dodecahedron, 2 of the 5 regular polyhedra.

 ## Expanded sphere

 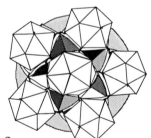 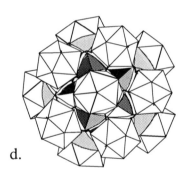

a. b. c. d.

a. Start with the icosadodecahedron sphere.
b. Make 12 icosahedra (3FA-44).
c. Six icosahedra placed into the inverted pentagon pyramids.
d. Sphere with all 12 pentagon pyramids filled in.
e. Any pentagon variation that is congruent, or less in length to the interval lengths of the sphere, will change the form of this pattern. Examples, (3FA-106-7).

e.

194

Short stellated icosadodecahedron

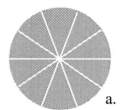
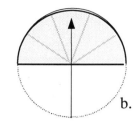
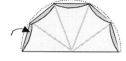

a. b. c. d.

a. Fold a 5-10 divided circle.
b. Fold it in half on any of the diameters.
c. Fold a line between each of the 10 points on the circumference. Do each fold separately.
d. Bring the edges of the 2 halves of the diameter around, folding on the creases, forming a pentagon pyramid. Tape the edges together.
e. Make 12 pyramids in this manner and tape them on to the pentagon spaces of the icosadodecahedral sphere.

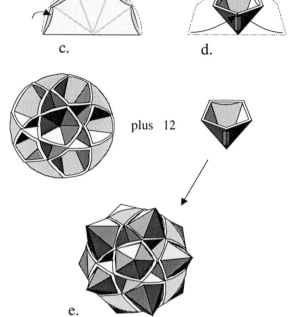

plus 12

e.

Long stellated icosadodecahedron

Make 20 extended triangles (3F –50a-q). Tape or glue triangles to each triangular interval on the sphere.

 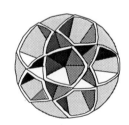 

twenty   plus   makes

Long and short stellated icosadodecahedron

Twelve pentagon pyramids plus 20 triangular pyramids attached to corresponding faces on the icosadodecahedron sphere combines both the icosahedron and dodecahedron pattern. Attach string connecting the points of the pentagon stellations. Do the same connecting the triangles giving linear form to the pattern.

3rd level pentagon development

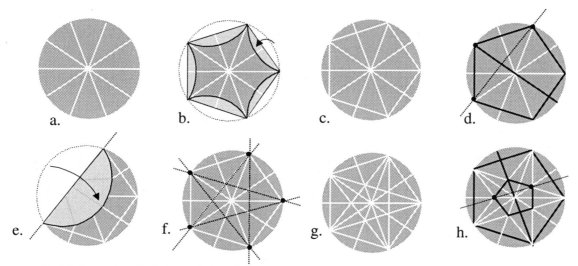

a. Fold the 5-10 division of the circle.
b. Fold the segment between every second point on the circumference towards the center forming the pentagon shape, one of 2 pentagons that are there.
c. Unfold circle. One pentagon becomes primary. The other 5 points function as bisectors. Each diameter functions as a primary pentagon point on one end and a bisector point on the opposite end.
d. Using only the 5 pentagon points, do as before, fold a diagonal line between every second point (This is exactly what we did in folding the 3-6 and 4-8 grids.)
e. As you make the fold notice how the points on the circumference line up with creased lines. There is much information to be observed about the pentagon by paying attention to the relationships revealed as you fold.
f. Fold all 5 diagonals. Give attention to developing alignment of points and folds.
g. Look at the pentagon star and divisions of all the creases. The right-triangle is primary to the pentagon just as it is to the hexagon and square.
h. Notice the orientation of the small pentagon formed by the crossing of the diagonals. To be consistent with this process, the center pentagon must be divided as the first, a line through every other point forming yet another smaller pentagon star.

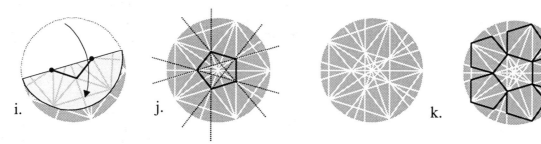

i. Fold the diagonal between points defining small pentagon.
j. Repeat this with all 5 diagonals. Look at symmetry of folds.
k. Find the 5 regular pentagons extending from the center pentagon

Dodecahedron solid

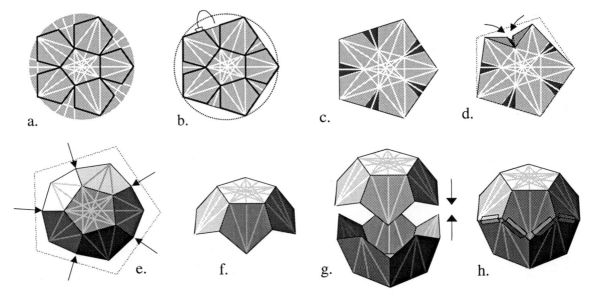

a. Fold the pentagon grid showing the 6 congruent pentagons.
b. Fold circumference to the back forming the pentagon shape.
c. Notice the crease down the middle between the pentagons.
d. Fold in on the center crease bringing the edges of the two adjacent pentagons together. Tape flaps in the back to hold them together.
e. Fold all 5 intervals to the back bringing the 5 pentagons together around the center pentagon.
f. The angles formed by the pentagons are the angles for the pentagons to form a spherical pattern.
g. Put 2 circles formed in this way together, edge to edge.
h. Tape the edges to close the dodecahedron.

Reconfiguration of pentagon

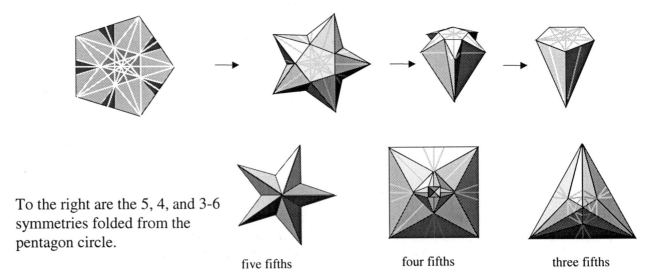

To the right are the 5, 4, and 3-6 symmetries folded from the pentagon circle.

five fifths   four fifths   three fifths

Cube dodecahedron

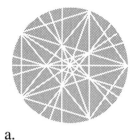
a.

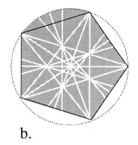
b.

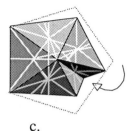
c.

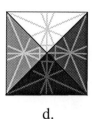
d.

e.

f.

a. Start with a level three folded grid.
b. Fold flaps over, forming the pentagon.
c. Fold in one-fifth of the pentagon.
d. This forms a square pyramid. Tape inside.
e. Find the creased design of the square star.
f. Locate the small diamond shape in center.
g. Push diamond in, bringing edges together.
h. Tape the edges closed. It is now a square with 2 top points where all 5 raised edges are the same length.

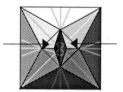
g.

h.

tape on both sides

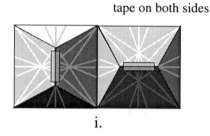
i.

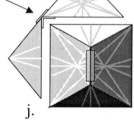
j.

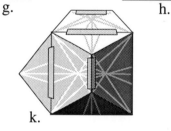
k.

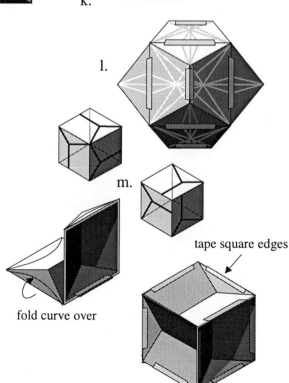

l.

m.

fold curve over

tape square edges

i. Make 2 units the same way. Place a square edge of each together with top edges perpendicular to each other, and tape along edges. Tape the edges with the square openings at right-angles to each other.
j. Place another square in the opening of the 2 squares taped at a right-angle to each other.
k. Tape along the edges. The 3 squares form the corner and 3 sides of a cube, at the same time making 3 pentagon shapes.
l. Three more units joined edge to edge in the same way, when joined to the first 3 will form the 6 squares making a cube, at the same time completing dodecahedron.
m. Reform the cube with the squares inside out. Make sure the triangle sides are next to the quadrilateral sides of each other. Fold curved flaps to the inside and tape before assembly.

Rhombicdodecahedron

a. Start by folding a level three pentagon in the circle, fold to pentagon shape.
b. Fold in one-fifth of the pentagon to form a square pyramid.

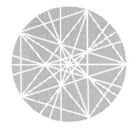

a.

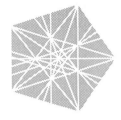

b.

c. Make 6 of these units and put them together in a cube pattern.
d. Tape on the edges which defines the cubic pattern. The form is a rhombicdodecahedron.

c.

d.

Here is a wonderful relationship between the square formed from 5-fold symmetry and the cube and rhomboid dodecahedron (3FA-14). This embodies both the tetrahedron and the octaheron.

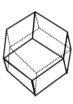

Variations in square pyramid

Below are folded variations by reforming the square pyramid to a 2 pointed pyramid (5FA-10a-h) through systematic pushing in and out on the folded lines. There are many combinations of design possibilities when using both sides of the folded circle.

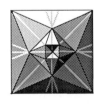

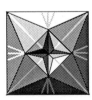

Penrose tiles

The Penrose tiles are 2 differently proportioned parallelograms that fill a plane with a 5-10 symmetrical pattern. It is a 10-point division of the circle in a star form.

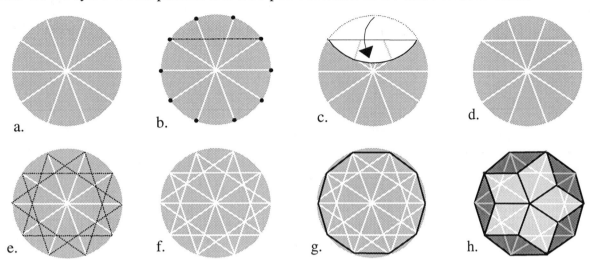

a. Start with the 5-10 division of the circle
b. Find a line connecting every fourth point.
c. Fold a crease connecting every other 2 points.
d. Skipping every 2 points covers 3/10 of the circle.
e. Connect every point to every third point by folding a line.
f. There are now 5 sets of 3 parallel lines forming a decastar.
g. Fold a line between every point on the circumference making a decagon.
h. Here we find two rhomboids that divide the decagon into a pentastar form.

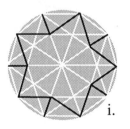 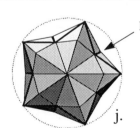 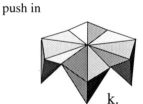 

i. Open circle and find the middle folds in the outer 5 rhomboids.
j. Push in on folds all the way around.
k. Continue to push lines under forming a rippled decagon surface with star point ends facing down.
l. Fold another the same way and put them together with star points of one fitting into the triangular intervals of the other. This is the same procedure as putting 2 half-open tetrahedra together to form an octahedron (3FA-11).

201

4th level pentagon development

  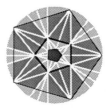 

level one
1 size pentagon

level two
2 size pentagons

level three
3 size pentagons

level four
5 size pentagons

Frequency does not describe the development of the pentagon grid. The diameters do not progressively divide into equal sections as in the 3-6 and 4-8 grids. The 5-10 grid generates a golden ratio growth proportion (p. 44, 193), that scales endless into and out from the pentagon pattern.

The use of the term "level" is to distinguish between coherent stages of pentagon development to the number of different size pentagons formed at each stage. Level one is the single pentagon. Level two shows 2, level three shows 3, and level four shows 5 different size regular pentagons.

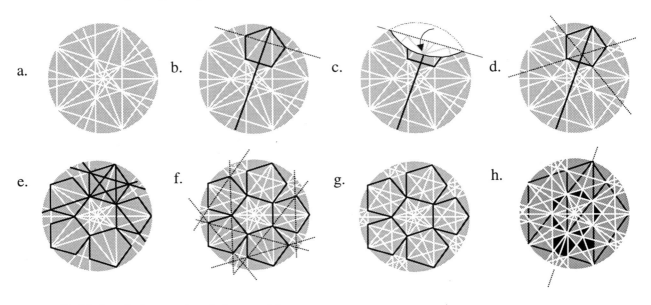

a. Fold the circle to a level three grid.
b. Locate an outside pentagon and find the diagonal perpendicular to the diameter.
c. Fold circumference over between the two points on the pentagon.
d. Fold the remaining 2 diagonals to complete the pentastar in that pentagon.
e. These lines begin to form the stars of pentagons to each side.
f. Continue folding diagonal to other pentagons to complete the stars.
g. All 6 pentagons have complete pentagon stars.
h. The five sizes of regular pentagons in grid level four.

Fractal development, 5-10

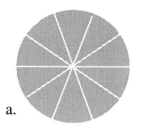
a.

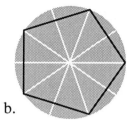
b.   1st level

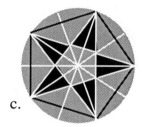
c.   2nd level

a. Fractal growth is a consistent development of information inherent to the proportional division of 5 diameters.

b. One of the 2 pentagons is formed.

c. A smaller pentagon is formed by the diagonals which make the star.

d. Folding the diagonal star of the smaller pentagon reveals a yet smaller centered pentagon. The pentagon of the first star now has 5 more pentagons of the same size off of each edge length with 2 diagonals already folded.

e. Folding diagonals in each of the 5 second size pentagons reveals more third level pentagons and generates another interval size pentagon.

f. By continuing to fold the diagonal stars, each level of newly formed pentagons will generate more pentagons to endless scale.

d.   3rd level

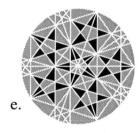
e.   4th level

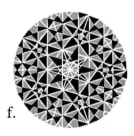
f.   5th level

Fractal development continued, 3-6

The nature of folding the circle is a fractal process. Fractal design is a function of the consistency of the folded grid. Proportion and frequency of division determines both diverse and similar kinds of forming.

The 4-frequency 3-6 grid reveals information to be able to change from half-divisions into folding thirds, thus going from 4-frequency to a 12-frequency diameter grid. It is within the 12-frequency grid that the standard images of fractal growth are to be found. The 1/3 folding is not covered in this book. It is in the circle to be found.

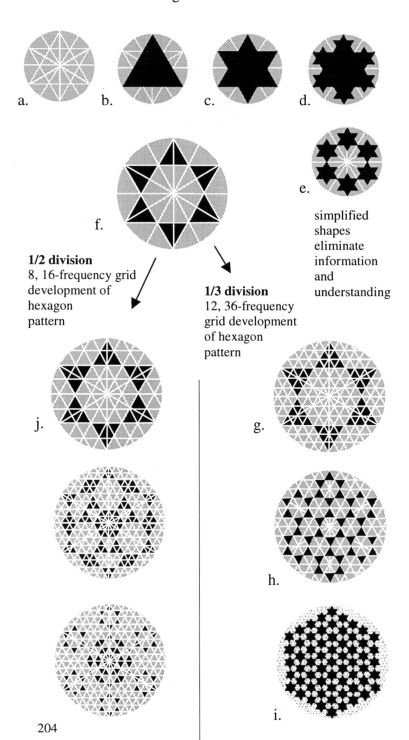

a. 4- frequency 3-6 grid.
b. Triangle isolated from grid.
c. Second level fractal development is hexagon star part of grid.
d. Third level fractal development occurs in 12-frequency grid (h).
e. Second level hexagons outlined on third level design revealing center.
f. The 4-frequency hexagon pattern is a juncture for continued grid folding of 1/2 or 1/3 divisions.
g. Second level fractal image (c) in 12-frequency grid.
h. Third level fractal image as it is found in 12-frequency grid (e).
i. Fourth level fractal formed in 36-frequency diameter grid.
j. Shows development of hexagon pattern in 8 and 16-frequency grids. The designs reflect proportional differences that generate different relationships within a given pattern.

These images represent design elements of patterned growth that occur in space observed in all natural formations; demonstrated in the folding and in-out reforming of the circle grid.

Fractal development continued, 4-8

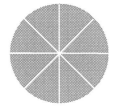 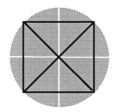 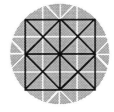 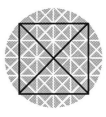

     Fractal growth is not evident in the 4-8 square grid as it is in the 5-10 and 3-6 grids. In the hexagon and pentagon grids the diagonals form a star around a center shape the same as that on the circumference. The inner and outer shapes are in opposite orientation because of the complimentary angles of intersecting diagonals. This produces a reflection of the same shape throughout with consistent division to the grid pattern which increases the number of parallel lines (see p.44).

     The diagonal intersection of the square at the center in the circle does not produce a star or central shape as the other two grids. In the square the diagonal is the diameter. In the pentagon and hexagon the two functions are separate lines of division which allow for off-centered angles to form the center shapes. While all other fractal qualities of the three grid patterns are the same, the angles of diagonal intersection are different. This goes back to the first fold of the circle being a right angle movement.

     The fractal nature of the square is in the form of the 2-frequency tetrahedral pattern (3FA-9). The 4-frequency diameter/diagonal image is an edge view compression of the tetrahedron and octahedron. Compound angles are distorted and space is lost in the flat image. In the 3-6 grid the tetrahedral compressed image is seen from a point view symmetry (3FA-15). The hexagon-patterned grid holds the fractal nature of both the square and the pentagon; all inherently the nature of circle/sphere wholeness.

Part 4

     The following photographs are of work made by the author. They are all made by folding and combining paper plates. These sculptural expressions use the principles and the process demonstrated in this book. Most of the work is glued together, has two coats of glue size and two coats of gesso, often with a finish coat of paint. They are very durable and light weight.

     These pictures were taken with a Casio LCD Digital Camera QV-10A, and processed through Corel Photo-Paint 5.0 .

above: Detail of "Grain". 6 feet 3 inches high
*   115 9" paper plates,*

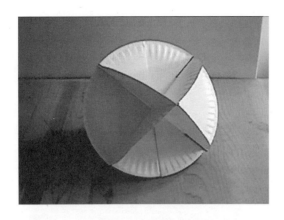
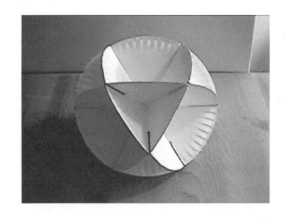

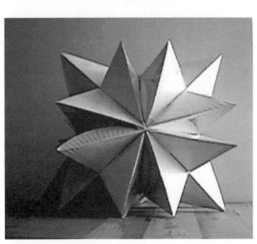
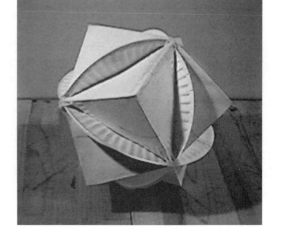

top left	Spherical Octahedron 4 9"paper plates (4FA-2)
top right	Spherical Cuboctahedron 4 9"paper plates (3FA-3)
center left	Spherical Icosadodecahedron 6 9" paper plates (5FA-2)
center right	Stellated Cuboctahedron 18 9" paper plates
bottom left	Stellated faces of stellated Octahedron 36 9" paper plates
bottom right	Stellated Octahedron 12 9" paper plates (4FA-10)

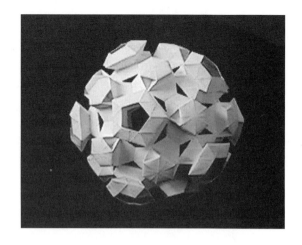

top left	Startree, upper portion detail
	174 9" paper plates
top right	Icosidodecahedral patterned sphere
	42 9" paper plates
above right	Great stellated dodecahedron
	22 9" paper plates (3FA-9)
bottom left	Stellated icosadodecahedron sphere
	38 9" paper plates (5FA-6)

top left	Hexagon/pentagon sphere, 20 9" paper plates
top right	Benzene Star, 109 9" paper plates (3FA-89)
center	Icosahedron sphere, 20 9" paper plates (3FA-88)
bottom	Crustacean, 42 9" paper plates

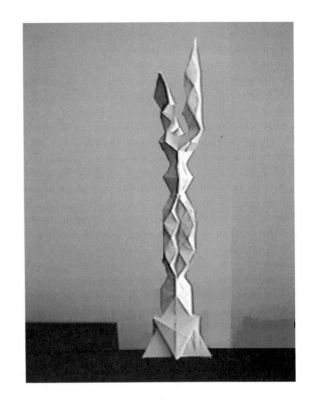

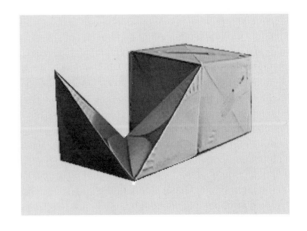

top left	Crossing 35 9" paper plates
top right	Flame 13 9" paper plates
bottom left	Blue moon 34 6" and 9" paper plates
bottom right	One and one half cube 6 9" paper plates

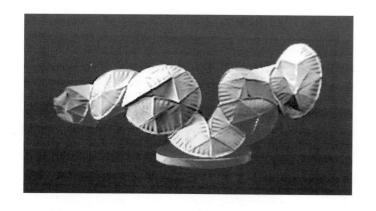
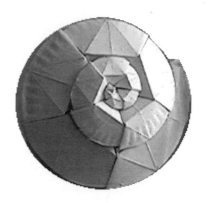

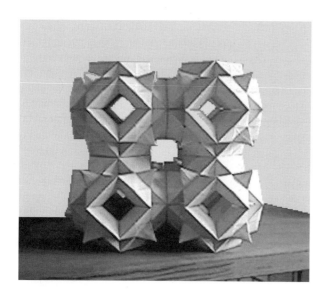

top left	Circle wave 33 9" paper plates (3FA-77)
top right	Spiral 13 9" paper plates (3FA-57)
center left	Icosahedral sphere 40 9" paper plates
center right	Spiral with tooth 18 9" paper plates (3FA-57)
bottom left	Cubic pattern 64 9" paper plates (3FA-82)

left   Inside/outside dodecahedron cube
22 9" paper plates (5FA-10, 12)
right   Mostly Feminine 49 9" paper plates

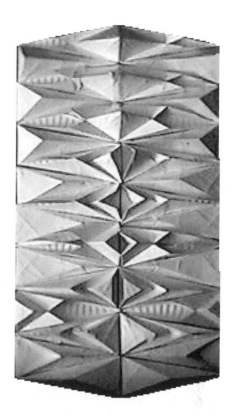

left   Male 68 9" paper plates

above Wall hanging 34 9" paper plates
(3FA-52)
below Twist 27 9" paper plates

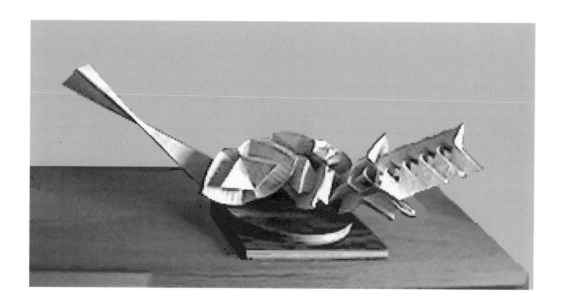

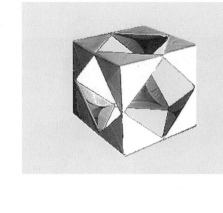

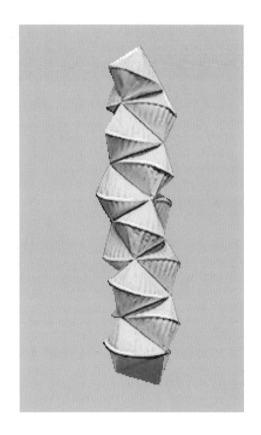

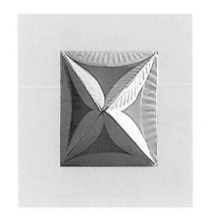

top left	Icosahedron pattern	20 9" paper plates
top right	Open cube	8 9" paper plates (4FA-18)
center left	Icosidodecahedron ball	32 9" paper plates
center right	Tetrahelix	16 9" paper plates (3FA-37.4)
bottom left	Octahedron	8 9" paper plates (4FA-3)

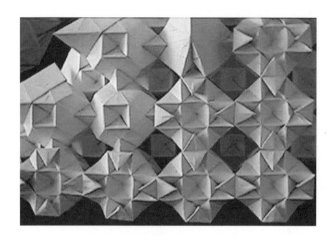
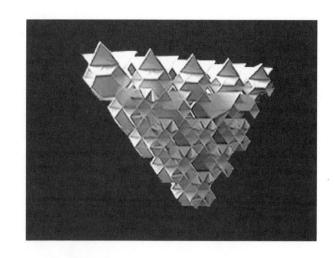
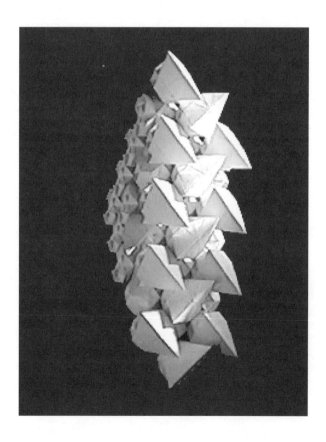

top right	Corner 102 9" paper plates
top left	Corner, detail
bottom right	Corner, end view
bottom left	Corner, side view

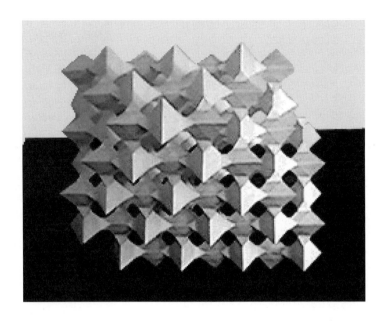

above   Benzene Matrix 84 9" paper plates (3FA-89)

left   Benzene Matrix, another view

bottom   Benzene Matrix, close-up

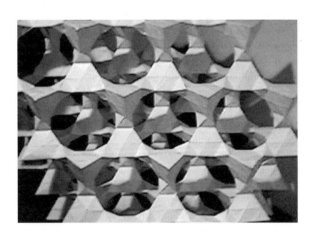

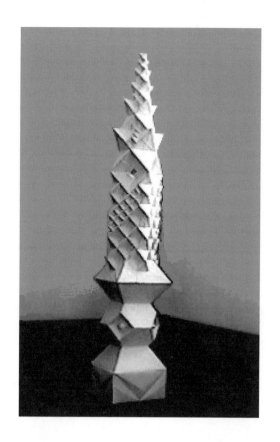
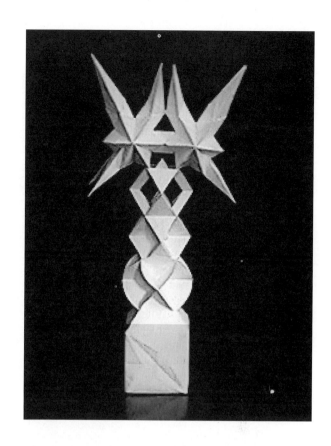

top left	Fractal tower 103 9" paper plates (3FA-27)
top right	African 65 9" paper plates
bottom left	Surge 43 9" paper plates
bottom right	Icosahedral sphere 80 9" paper plates (3FA-80)

top   Bird   35   6" and 9" paper plates

bottom   Con I   23   9" paper plates

SELECTECTED BIBLIOGRAPHY

The Geometrical Foundation of Natural Structure by Robert Williams (Dover Publications, Inc., 1972)

Universal Patterns by Rochelle Newman & Martha Boles (Pythagorean Press, 1992)

Shapes, Space, and Symmetry by Alan Holden (Dover Publications, Inc., 1971)

Patterns in Nature by Peter S. Stevens (Alantic Little, Brown and Co., 1974)

Order in Space by Keith Critchlow (The Vicking Press, 1970)

Crystal & Dragon by David Wade (Destiny Books, 1993)

Time Stands Still by Keith Critchlow (St. Martin's Press, 1982)

The Reflective Universe by Arthur M. Young (Robert Briggs Associates, 1976)

Space Grid Structures by John Borrego (MIT Press, 1968)

Chaos by James Gleick (Penguin Books, 1987)

The Secret of Light by Walter Russell (University of Science and Philosophy, 1947)

Stalking the Wild Pendulum by Itzhak Bentov (E.P. Dutton, 1977)

Education & the Significance of Life by Krishnamurti (Harper San Francisco, 1953)

Unfolding Meaning by David Bohm (ARK Paperbacks, 1985)

Wholeness and the Implicate Order by David Bohm (Routedge & Kegan Paul, 1980)

The Sense of Unity by Nader Ardalan & Laleh Bakhtiar (The University of Chicago, 1973)

Islamic Patterns by Keith Critchlow (Schocken Books, 1976)

Cymatics, (book 1 and book 2) by Hans Jenny (Bsailius Presse Basel, 1974)

The Geometry of Art and Life by Matila Ghyka (Dover Publications, Inc., 1977)

The Timless Way of Building by Christopher Alexander (Oxford University Press, 1979)

Geometry in Architecture by William Blackwell A.I.A. (Key Curriculum Press, 1984)

The Cosmic Crystal Sprial by Ra Bonewitz (Element Books, 1986)

Synergetics by R. Buckminster Fuller (Macmillian Publishing Co., Inc., 1975)

Synergetics 2 by R. Buckminster Fuller (Macmillian Publishing Co., Inc., 1979)

The Discovery of the Child by Maria Montessori (Kalakshetra Publications, 1966)

The Findhorn Garden by the Findhorn Community (Harper Colophon Books, 1975)

The Urantia Book (Urantia Foundation, 1955)

How to Build a Flying Saucer by T. B. Pawlicki (Prentice-Hall, Inc., 1981)

New Light On Space and Time by Dewey B Larson (Reciprocity Publishers, 1965)

Inventing Kindergarten by Norman Brosterman (Harry Abrams, Inc., 1997)

about the author

Bradford Hansen-Smith lives in Chicago and works as an independent consultant in Chicago area schools from elementary to college level. He works in the classroom and does teacher in-service workshops. His life as a sculptor brought him to an involvement in exploring the geometry of spatial patterns. He has received three US patents for the development of applications that have come out of his work with geometric movement systems. This is his second book resulting from ten years of folding and joining paper circles. A modeling process has emerged that is informational to basic patterns and forms that are taught in many areas of our educational curriculum. The most obvious connections are made in the area of Mathematics and Geometry.

He is concerned about how we educate each other that have led us to an unbalanced planetary condition, and a general disrespect for life. He feels the circle is an important tool that can offer insights into shifting awareness towards more comprehensive concerns. By understanding the reality of wholeness as a critical element in being able to identify the necessary connections, he feels we can recreate healthy conditions for all life.